LENNY, FLIP, AND RICKLES
Standup Comics In The Magic City

by Jacob Katel

Some of the Other Books I Wrote

- Cuban Coffee Windows of Miami
- A People's History of Overtown Vol. 1
- Hidden Springs Of The Everglades
- Watery Miami
- Miami Grime Fiction

PROLOGUE

THE CONNECTICUT PARTY RECORD RAIDS OF 1962

Pearl Williams, Belle Barth, and B.S. Pully, "Brought about the arrest of nine record retailers and distributors in six Connecticut cities," according to a front page story in the Meriden Journal on February 5, 1962. It all started with "A Trip Around The World Is Not A Cruise," by Pearl Williams. The newspaper editors heard it, and were such lame dorks they set out to ruin the fun.

"Throughout both sides of the record there were the most open, to the point descriptions of erotic situations. There were repeated references to male and female sexual organs. The record was laced with gutter jokes about homosexuality and unnatural sex acts. Religious and nationality groups were the frequent object of ridicule. There seemed to be no issue of freedom of speech involved here. There didn't seem to be any way the performances could be arguable as works of art."

Damn.

The newspaper fully investigated the manufacture and distribution of the Surprise and After Hours record labels, their corporate structure, their distributors, and their retail outlets, employing regional bureaus to cast a wider surveillance net. After publishing, the newspaper turned over all the information they'd collected to the authorities. The fuzz used it to, "Conduct synchronized raids by state and municipal police. Arrests were made under a state obscenity statute. State police estimate that close to 6,000 of the records by relatively unknown comedians Pearl Williams, Belle Barth, and B.S. Pully were seized in the raids in the communities of Meriden, Southington, Wallingford, Hartford, East Hartford, and Hamden."

And that's how freedom of the press was used to violate freedom of expression courtesy of illegal search and seizure. Three amendments in one. But it was nothing new for Belle Barth.

She was arrested for obscenity on Miami Beach in 1953.

And in 1961, the Los Angeles Vice Squad arrested Belle at the Cloister Club (8588 Sunset Blvd, just three tenths of a mile from the future Comedy Store). Arrested her after a 2a.m. show, booked her at West Hollywood substation, and released her on $525 bail on "Suspicion of performing a lewd show where she uses Anglo Saxon four letter words and obscene gestures as part of her comedy routine."

Barth's only comment, "If I embarrass you dearie, tell your friends."

On February 18, 1961, Judge Adolph Alexander of Beverly Hills Municipal Court dismissed the charge because Belle had been charged with the wrong section in the penal code. Penal code is when a lady writes her number on his schmuck. How's that for a punchline

TONIGHT

LENNY BRUCE

PAYS TRIBUTE TO

BELLE BARTH

Bel-Aire Hotel

SHOWTIMES: 10 - 12 - 2

6515 Collins
Ave., M.B.

UN 6-3262

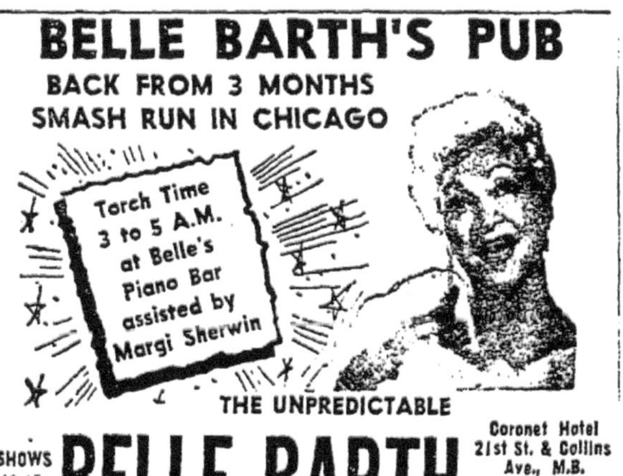
BELLE BARTH'S PUB
BACK FROM 3 MONTHS
SMASH RUN IN CHICAGO
Torch Time
3 to 5 A.M.
at Belle's
Piano Bar
assisted by
Margi Sherwin
THE UNPREDICTABLE
SHOWS
10:15
12:15
BELLE BARTH
Coronet Hotel
21st St. & Collins
Ave., M.B.
FOR RES.:
JE 1-3733

BELLE BARTH

Belle Barth was an American standup comic who spoke dirty Yiddish ghetto lingo flavored in the fatty schmaltz of her own irreverence, with big, fat, hard, long consonants dripping wet in double talk and innuendo. Her birth name was Annabelle Salzman, but she was Belle Barth (pronounced Bart) to the world. A platinum recording artist getting ripped off for her party records by the authorities as well as gangsters in the music business, a powerful category in the mix of creative entrepreneurs who put the audio from live standup into living rooms on hi fi's everywhere. Records made Belle famous, but it was her live show that made her nut. Live shows meant cash. And cash is how she made her money. She was a crowd-work heavyweight, and heckler exterminator. Had a big funny laugh like a broadsword to cut up the audience at the end of her lines. A hammer's wit fired eye level from close range, under low ceilings, with spotlights blazing. Smoke everywhere. Watta ya this. Watta ya that. Tons of written material fought with her first reactions to funny faces. Jokes ran streaming consciousness through raging river rapids of her improvised riffology to see who got to the punchline first. She shredded goofs on sight. A bully with a juicy knish for big resounding bully bits, with her machine gun backup piano finely tuned in on the pulse of her rhythm and fucking the room into acute live show psychosis. Midnight? Is that all you got? Fuhgettaboutit, try 2, 3, 4, 5a.m. shows. On the regular. Everybody rocking thwacked out on the beach on dexxies, and bennies, and blackies, and greenies, and reds, and pure codeine syrup purchased over the counter at every drug store if you couldn't get junk, and all kinds of liquor, some of it moonshine, and big fat Cuban cigars aged in Havana, and you just hit the numbers, and your pockets were fat, and so was the lady on stage, just owning the hilarious movie called now. Had some creepy level psychic read on every room. Mothafuckas intuition. The singular consciousness of a show in a box on a rock in space on a parabola through your doors of perception. With the help of liquor, comedy exploded through the crowd as involuntary spasms of psychedelic laugh magic. Throughout her decades in showbiz, people shit, pissed, farted, gave birth, were born, and died during her sets. The whole dang human comedy. Barth was in your face, lovable, offensive, and arrestable. The times they put her in steel bracelets. She had a temper. A loud mouth. A microphone. Inspiration. Earned on decades of nightly live performances all over Miami, Chicago, NYC, and Las Vegas, including at her own club, called Belle Barth's Pub in the Coronet Hotel at 21st and Collins Ave on Miami Beach. A long way up for a high school dropout. She started working Vaudevilles in the 1920's. Belle Barth was a broad in charge and full of dirty Ukrainian shtetl humor. The very same low down type of dirty talk as La Wanda Page and Moms Mabley, just a different dialect. Big evil laugh. Like a ghoul ate a goblin. Dark and mirthful. Belle Barth's main subjects were sex, money, relationships, and the crowds in her audience; distorted through her comedic lens, propelled by musical accompaniment by her old pal Margi Sherwin on the keys. Claiming she could line a hundred men up against a wall, and bet a hundred dollars she could bang them all, which kicks off her classic and widely distributed party album, "If I Embarrass You, Tell Your Friends," recorded in front of a live nightclub audience at her shingle on Miami Beach, released in 1960 on the After Hours label. It's hard to track the numbers, cause the record company hid them, but the most popular party / novelty records going back to Redd Foxx, sold millions. After Hours was an underground and mostly under the counter label with shadowy origins and all identifying info obfuscated from its graphics. It had national distribution and a dark money promo budget. While she had been heavily advertised in major newspapers for years in the comedy capitals, in a single three month span of first quarter sales, her voice finally reached the recesses of America. Great promo. But it came at the cost of her residuals. The album shocked and titillated squares. An underground hit. Belle was from a hard rocking all night party life, and even though she had a strange and even Jewish perspective, the album captured a large black and white American audience for its novelty, laugh quotient, the risqué concepts of a female orgasm, shitting your pants, and schmucks. The art of standup comedy for all to hear. Freedom of speech, American style. Pulled up from under the dusty back counters of record stores in all the states that counted. States of confusion, intoxication, and delirium included. In 1962, an obvious spaghetti vendor named Manlio Severino conspired to bootleg this album in a pretty sophisticated counterfeiting network and got sued for it. Shoulda stuck to red sauce. In 1963, Barth took the labels After Hour Records and Roulette Records to Federal Court for ripping her off, even the famous mobster-owned Roulette Records' Moshe Levy, for her "Live At The Roundtable" album recorded at his Vinny "The Chin" Gigante affiliated outpost in NYC. Morris Levy from Roulette was a cutthroat with a catalog. He beat John Lennon in court for fucks sakes. Sure the labels ripped Belle off. Comedy's always been a dirty business. LAFF Records allegedly generally paid their artists $100 with no back end. Richard Pryor? They used old drug addled contracts to record and press up bootlegged sets of him working out material in lousy clubs, then timed their releases to coincide with his official projects on major labels. A comic's nightmare. That's why Flip Wilson was so smart to do his Little David Records label. He owned his masters, writers, and publishing, the holy trifecta of the music business, which is where comedy albums fall into. Albums were nothin' but matza crackers to Belle Barth, and she had to make her bread rise. For her it was all about the club. Because live shows meant cash. And cash is how she made her money. So even though she lost out on record profits, she made more for performing, and the vinyl sales promoted her and raised her rate and profile. Brought her heat from the coppers too. But if she shoulda got maybe a penny or a nickel off each record sale, she was maybe owed ten to fifty thousand dollars for every million sold. She was a sharp lady after all, but the company still did a lot for her. The mob had its own recording, mixing, mastering, artwork, pressings, which took lines of credit with the pressing plants; packaging, distributors, shipping for large quantity vinyl by planes, trains, and automobiles, and then of course collecting the money at the end of the quarter, and receiving the ten percent product that always came back, it being the retail business. All that is a lot of work. You ever seen a room with a million records in it? The comic didn't have the infrastructure for it at the time. The labels made it happen. Even Flip Wilson made a deal for Little David through Atlantic's distribution. Now, it's different. Anybody can do anything at the touch of a phone. The Mafia did a lot for comedy. They really did. God Bless the Italian-American community for that. As for her live show, you can hear Belle riffing and cracking and ranking on Jews, Italians, Irish, sexuality, poop, suicide, marriage, and how to fart instead of cough so's not to interrupt the show, "Reverse it!" in front of tourists, locals, regulars, virgins, drunks, and comedy hounds alike. Nobody got hurt. Belle Barth's Pub was alive, as you can hear, with glasses clinking, tables knocking, people laughing and coughing and smoking, falling out, cracking up, chiming in and elbowing each other in good, clear, well engineered audio. The beachfront drunken sandy grit of sweet intoxication. The voracious revelry of friction chaffing all the sweat up in that fucked up funny jungle of the Florida heat. A howling document of language, diction, style, and substances. The Rocking MB where Flip Wilson, and George Kirby worked out was right around the corner. And Murray Franklin's, where Don Rickles got started was right there too, those 20th to 23rd streets off Collins Ave. Little Liberty Ave area. Place Pigalle. B.S. Pully. Sophie. Rickles. Flip. Frank.

Dean. Pearl. Belle, she was in the streets with all them. Probably ran into each other like comics do. Probably went to Wolfie's Diner with all the bartenders, chorus girls, comics, musicians, and strippers leaving work; and all the old Jews waking up. Get out of the club, and hit about three more bars, Zissen's Bowery, Charlie's Inn, The Tahiti, or the bar at the Netherlands Hotel, before heading back to an ice cold air conditioned suite. Go to sleep at 2p.m and back to work at 8 or 9 or 10 at night. Do it all again. That's how it was. Barth was born in 1911 and grew up in Manhattan working different clubs and hotels on the Borscht Belt, the Jewish comedy route, like a chitlin circuit but for matzoh balls. She was the ninth kid in her family and got married five times, and one of the husbands, she kept his last name cause it went better. Moved to South Beach in 1950. Started working. Bam. 1953, she was arrested by Florida Beverage Agents for obscenity; singing dirty songs at the Music Box Lounge at the Hotel Good, 4301 Collins Ave, according to the Miami Herald. Milton "Uncle Miltie" Sackett, the operator of the bar got busted right along with her and booked into Miami Beach Police Station for, "Permitting and maintaining a nuisance which tends to corrupt morals." The whole thing smelled funny from the start. Belle was charged with, "Performing in an indecent manner." They each got released on

$75 bond and were later fined $25 by Judge Leonard Saperstein, who refused Barth's lawyer's argument to compare lyrics to literature or comedy to art. I declare his objection overruled. Somebody call Pigmeat Markham. Here come da judge. Ultimately, the bar received a thirty day suspension on its liquor license. Ouch. State Beverage Director and obvious ball juggler J.H. Hunter said it was because of the, "Lewd, wanton, and lascivious performance by a female entertainer who performs in a suggestive, vulgar, and indecent manner." Milton Sackett was the bar operator. He was found guilty of disorderly conduct and maintaining a nuisance. He was an interesting cat. See, he moved to Miami Beach in 1947 and was an MC for 27 years and owned or operated 15 different lounges on the beach. He was a New Yorker who helped build ships during WWII. And he helped Belle Barth build her career too. He died of a heart attack in 1973. When he died, he was the operator of the Golden Vee in the Cadillac Hotel. He and Belle were arrested by bumbling Beverage Agents Louis Emmons and Thomas Barger, who came to court prepared with a tape they had recorded in the club to make their case. The judge tossed out their audio for being garbled. However, Saperstein took their testimony at face value about what happened. Belle did not sit down to take the stand, why would she it's oxymoronic, though maybe her charismatic presence could have swayed the judge. A fellow Jew, no less. Perhaps if Barth had appealed, she would've won a landmark case. Her acquiescence tends to bury the case historically, but it was certainly easier for her at the time. The old adage that the lawyer gets all the money in the end probably having something to do with it. She paid the fine and kept it moving. Adapted her act with even more cussing and profanity, but in her unintelligible-to-white-ears Yiddish double talk. Make no mistake. She was unpredictable. Lenny Bruce was a fan of Belle Barth and did a tribute show to her at the Bel Aire Hotel in 1962. He knew that she had run the gauntlet for her act. He respected her. Plus, Lenny's entertainer mom wrote his act in the very beginning. So he had a soft spot for funny ladies. They probably knew each other. Maybe even back in New York. They were ilk. Club comics. Belle Barth passed away at home on Miami Beach on Valentine's Day 1971. Some of the places she performed in Miami were the 5 O'Clock Club, the Mayflower Lounge, Dore's Supper Club, the Saxony Rooftop, Copa City, Harry's American Bar at The Eden Roc, Mother Kelly's, the Balkan Room at The Atlantis Hotel, and of course at her own place, Belle Barth's Pub. She was a top tier headliner at Caesar's Palace Las Vegas, and Carnegie Hall in New York City. Imagine Belle in 1959 and in her prime, big funny laughing face lighting up the beach. Torch time 3a.m. to 5a.m. Belle's Piano Bar, assisted by Margi Sherwin. Real comic. Check the progression of her sets from the first show all the way through the 5a.m. show on her live albums. It's as good a document of the art of standup comedy as anything that's come along since she got to Miami in 1950. Long live Belle Barth.

RESERVE NOW FOR
NEW YEAR'S EVE

LENNY
BRUCE

SHOW TIME 10:00-1:00
Saturday 10:00 - 12:30 & 2:30

El Patio Supper Club

1405 DADE BLVD. • JE 8-6593

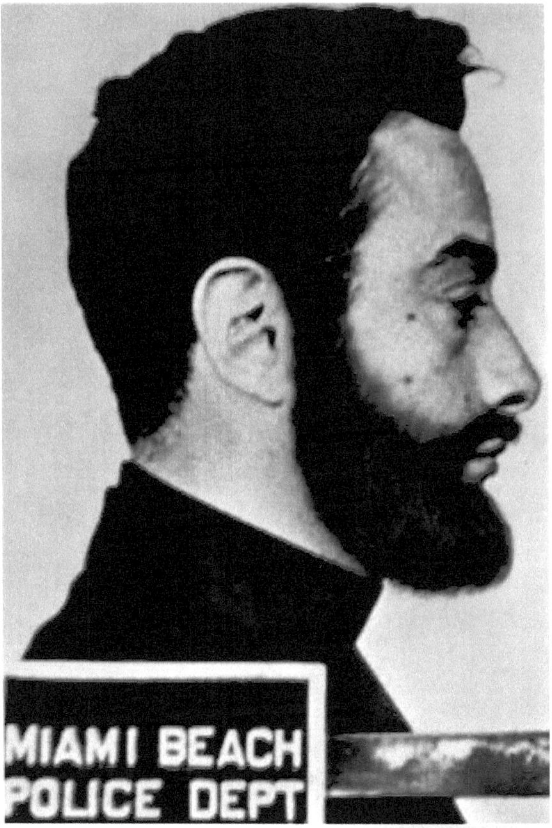

MIAMI BEACH
POLICE DEPT

Honey Harlow 1950

DON'T MISS

BEYOND THE LIMIT

WITH

ONE NIGHT ONLY
SATURDAY, AUG. 24

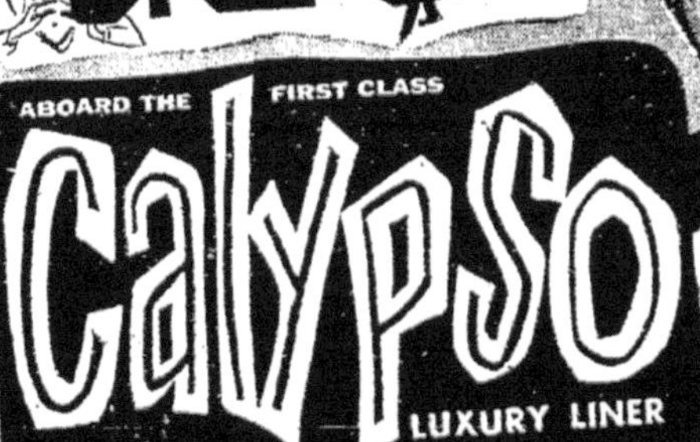

BOISTEROUS FUN
FUNNY
downright hilarious

SAT. NITE
MOONLITE
CRUISE
TO BIMINI AND BACK

$6.50 NO TAX
NO COVER — NO MINIMUM
ALL DRINKS 50c
1 FREE DRINK

For Information Reservations Calypso
JE 2-4477

DEPART 8:30 P.M. RETURN 2 A.M.
OVERNIGHT ACCOMMODATIONS AVAILABLE ON THIS CRUISE

GAMES

SNACK BAR - CLUB ENTERTAINMENT CALYPSO MUSIC - DANCING

MIAMI'S ONLY 100% STABILIZED COMPLETELY AIR CONDITIONED LINER

LENNY BRUCE

The year was 1963 and Lenny Bruce was America's most subversive communicator, according to his arrest record for standup comedy, and he was headlining a midnight moonlight cruise from Miami to Bimini, Bahamas, fifty miles due east from South Beach. So in the spirit of Bruce, let's imagine for a moment that he has a suit pocket full of pharmacy grade liquid methamphetamine hydrochloride in glass ampules. Pure speed from a doctor. He's got a hypodermic spike locked on a syringe, and a nylon parachute cord he got from a fellow war vet to tie off with. He's in the cruise ship bathroom cross-firing his soul up with a taste of the sweet hereafter, meth then heroin, and then shooting blood across the wall through his needle just for kicks. It's a hundred mile round trip boat ride and he don't wanna get seasick. Lenny's feeling good because he has a flock of quacked out stethoscopers around the country writing him scripts for everything from Dilaudid, to Tuinal, to Demerol, to Secanol, to Dexedrine, to Benzedrine, to Morphine; all those reds, blacks, greens, and most important, his all consuming shard rock crystal glass or liquid Methedrine, king over every upper, downer, mover, shaker, stopper, or dropper he can get his comic little hands on. Even heroin, which is a real treat for him, as all the jazz cats know. Even though they only know because it kills them all. By the end of it, his blasted and collapsed veins and subdural hematomatoes and staph infections, bacteria, fungus, scabs, pus, blood, grime and maybe Hep C, Tuberculosis, abscessing, cystic, necrotizing fasciitis rendered his naked visage a living breathing dying rotting corpse akimbo. A shell of a man who could not sleep, and would not wake. The contradiction in terms a metaphor for his zombie-like state. People tend to associate Lenny Bruce with heroin or morphine, what they say killed him when he nodded off while shooting dope on a toilet and then rung his bell for whom it tolled on cold hard porcelain tile. But it was all that pure legal mainline meth in his veins that kept Lenny going most of the time, in an impossible to sustain perceptual seizure of a waking schizophrenic paranoiac rage against the dying of the night. A dream turned nightmare flurry of illogical, irrational, extremes, which is what meth always leads to over time, in a race to self destruction. And his psyche tracked its course around a million mile an hour figure-eight loop of cops and prosecutors and judges who mostly made his life miserable with restricting his free speech as they undertook the trials of his tribulations. Man, life can be depressing for a comic without a mic or a stage.

Lenny Bruce was ahead of his time. Severe understatement.

That's why his infamy from yesterday keeps him famous today. Villain yesterday, hero tomorrow.

Somehow he still captures the world's imagination every time his name is mentioned. People don't usually talk about how funny he was, but he was hilarious. A fast talking magnetic charmer obsessed with wordplay.

Born to a Jewish stripper and a British vagabond, he was passed around hand to hand between relatives as his parent's marriage fell apart. He graduated elementary school, worked on a farm from the age 11, joined the U.S. Navy when he turned 16, and got sent off to fight in World War II. After the war, he worked in factories, as a theater usher, and working Merchant Marine ships between the U.S., Italy, Turkey, and China. He also took acting classes in California on the GI Bill.

He got started as a comic at a Brooklyn nightclub doing jokes for $12 a week. Then he won a national talent show from a big radio host named Arthur Godfrey. The victory came with paid gigs, and he found himself performing at downtown Miami's (still standing) Olympia Theater on Flagler Street way back on August 17, 1949. The show made it into the Miami Herald with a poster advertising the two-for-one stage and screen event with a Cuban harmonic trio called the DeCastro sisters as musical headliners, Lenny Bruce the "Young Man Of Distinction," a tap dancer, and a band, before a film called The Girl From Jones Beach, starring Ronald Reagan, played on the big screen.

Lenny got good reviews. It was a one-off. But he'd be back.

The way it happened is that he walked into a popular 24 hour diner, the Mayflower in Baltimore after a show, and he fell in love at first sight with the exotic dancer Honey Harlow.

Hot Honey Harlow. Beautiful red head.

They had a sex filled week of intense passion, but he had a work contract as a merchant marine for a voyage across the ocean, and he was leaving the U.S. for three months. They went their ways, but he was so hot for her that he sacrificed his month's pay and jumped ship in Spain to come back and meet her on Miami Beach. Honey was peel-dancing at the Paddock Club. According to her autobiography, called Honey: Lenny's Shady Lady, he flew in, they got it on better than she'd ever had, she broke up with the hot black lesbian woman she'd been fucking, and her and Lenny got connecting suites at the Floridian Hotel at 540 West Ave, Miami Beach. The place was built for $1.5 million in 1925, right off the 5th street causeway on the bay side of the island. And according to Honey Harlow in her book, "One of the few better hotels that allowed Jews." Yeah, there was a lot of places Jews weren't welcome back then.

They made love, partied, and hung out in the calm blue waves; Caught the sun between them, and its all-consuming power fused their twisted souls together like a live wire. The guardrail separating their psyche annihilated in ecstatic firestorms of lust as the racecars of their consci shot through the tunnels of each others' pupils simultaneously when they came. This was the early days of their wild life together. Before the car crash that cracked her pelvis in Pittsburgh, and almost killed her at the apex of her vixen stripper body's sexual peak of prowess.

Bruce and Honey were in love. They should've never left Miami Beach.

He was her handsome, high assed, fast talking genius. She was his ten thousand buck an hour Madonna-Whore. They had a complex relationship; and a relationship complex. Together they were inseparable. Lenny didn't want no louche and leering liver-spotted lowlifes fee-loading off his wife-to-be's bodacious buxom body, baby. But the beach was full of two bit comics and it was hard for him to find a gig. Meanwhile, Hot Honey Harlow was one of the biggest feature dancers in South Florida, made great money, and drove a canary yellow 1949 Chevy convertible with a hand-painted foot-high cartoon of her on the driver side door, wearing a G-string and nipple pasties with her red hair blowing in the breeze and her name spelled under it. Custom cheetah interior. Beautiful car. Lenny hated it.

He had to come up with a plan. How to make money fast. Without working.

He needed enough money to keep her clothes on, cause he wanted to marry Honey, and he didn't want his wife to be a stripper. He was gonna teach her to sing and they were gonna be on stage together making magic.

She was the love of his life, his baby's mother to be. So he developed a scam so cold he actually had to trade it to God as a chip from the Devil to save her life when she got run over; praying for her to live, he swore he'd never do it again.

The scam was called the Brother Matthias Foundation, Inc. a New York chartered not-for-profit corporation that was legally established in May of 1951 by Lenny Bruce, after a late night riff between he and his mother Sally Marr, the comedian Buddy Hackett, and some other comics, and is still active today as of 2023 according to New York state corporate records. The gimmick is that it wasn't a scam at all. It was charity. Totally legal, and yet somehow tainted. Hilarious bit though. You see, Lenny Bruce was a war hero who saw action at Casablanca and Salerno. He won a unit citation at Anzio, which is how he ended up on a leper colony in British Guiana while his ship was getting refitted with guns in 1944. Bruce had never heard of a leper before, let alone seen one with his own two eyes, and those poor noseless bastards with their limbs and flesh all rotting as they were sure did something to his heartstrings. Pulled them. So back in the states, he raised the means to send them a massive shipment of sunglasses, solar sensitivity being a leper's living nightmare, and the Detroit Free Press wrote him up for it in a feature article by veteran journalist Ralph Nelson, who said, "Off stage one of Lenny's serious interests is chairman of the Brother

Mathias Foundation, which aids the members of a leper colony in British Guiana."

So in 1951, while he was having trouble finding gigs as an unknown comic on Miami Beach with a hundred buck a day meth habit and the woman of his dreams to impress, he decided to reactivate the foundation's operations. He pretended to be a dry-clean pickup man and stole a priest's clothes from a Catholic church, then went door to door asking for donations. He made eight thousand dollars in three days, then got arrested for panhandling and vagrancy on 48th and Alton, which is still a rich area today and not far from Mt. Sinai Hospital where he almost died on the critical list in 1960 having rough ailments due to infections from injections. Anyway, when he was able to prove that his Brother Mathias Foundation was legit and that the leper colony existed, the judge let him go and dropped the charges.

The whole story is in his book, How To Talk Dirty and Influence People, along with his mugshot and arrest report. The scam's execution and profits are validated by Honey Harlow in her book. However, one thing is funny about the arrest report, which is ostensibly the genuine article, as it appears in his book. The arresting officer is listed as L.H. Oodood. Interesting name. Can't find it anywhere. I'm not saying anything besides what I'm saying, but all I'm saying is that "Oodood" is Doo-doo spelled backwards, and L.H. also adds up to Lenny Honey. Funny guy. Such a funny detail.

The lore is that Bruce cut a check for $2,500 to the forgotten lepers of the South Pacific, out there in Mahaicony Hospital, East Coast Demerara, British Guiana, and kept the rest of the money for operating expenses. Typical foundation.

After Lenny got busted, Honey Harlow got a call that her mom was sick back in Detroit so she flew home, and Lenny drove her car up with all their stuff a week later. They left Miami and that changed everything.

When Honey's mom got better, they went to Pittsburgh trying to make it as a magic act when their new car got t-boned on the passenger side by a Packard that was flying around a truck at high speed. Lenny was driving. The violent collision spun the car and threw Honey out the window and into the the intersection. The truck ran over her torso, leaving a bloody mangled mess of steel, flesh, and concrete.

Crying over her unconscious form, Lenny prayed to God that if he would save her life, he would give up the Brother Mathias Foundation work for good.

Thankfully, she survived. But by 1957, they had a one year old baby and a divorce.

It was a rough decade and it was about to get tougher. The marriage had crashed and burned just like the car did. In less than amicable circumstances. Honey was now a full-on addict just like him, or maybe even worse. All that pain. She needed nature's most potent painkiller. Heroin.

In January 1960, with his career on an upswing, Lenny was headlining at the El Patio Supper Club, back on South Beach at 14th and Dade. He was doing a midnight show followed by an extended preview of his new movie called The Leather Jacket. For a long time that's the only people who got to see it, cause the movie never got made. The footage is now available online. A movie that did get made is called Dance Hall Racket, and Lenny, Honey and Sally are all in it. It's a solid picture. As for the El Patio Supper Club, Lenny talked about it in a famous recorded performance, one of his last ever actually, out in San Francisco at a club called the Basin Street West. The set gets off to a slow start, but he loosens up around half way through and starts talking about Miami. He talks about the owner of the El Patio Supper Club, Sam "Barney" Barnett, "A huge, tough guy. Big guy, 6' 6", no neck, 330 pounds…a union organizer who beat the shit out of the Cubans, and made bus boys outta them….When Barney passed away, the bartenders didn't steal in case it was a trick." Then Lenny told a story about a hot night on Miami Beach when he was on stage riffing on integration. Four southerners in the audience didn't like his point of view. One of the chicks in the group got hostile and beamed an old fashioned tumbler at his forehead. The group rushed to leavebut the guy at the door was Barney, who was, "Born in South Philly, raised in The Bronx." Barney said, "Hey ya motherfucker why are you throwing glasses?" But, "It wasn't a question, just a preface for a lobotomy and a chest x-ray," said Lenny. Sam was a strong-arm with a strong arm. He was his own muscle. The group ran past him and jumped in a cab to escape. So Barney ran around to the cab driver's window and punched him out cold so they couldn't leave. That's the kind of place that El Patio Supper Club was. The guy was Samuel Barnett, also known as Sam. Lenny called him Barney; and Barney did business with the mob, who were all over Miami Beach and South Florida in general. Bruce liked working with criminals and characters like Barnett, and they liked him the same. Barney took such a liking to Bruce that he even fronted him

$25,000 for a down payment on his house in California in exchange for future performances. Lenny loved the El Patio Supper Club. His reputation in the underworld was established and respected. It was the damn established social disorder and the critics that kept trying to crush his soul. In 1963, Lenny was banned from Britain. Not for anything he did there. Just for the energy around his name. Officials decided that, "It would not be in the public interest to allow him into the country." Supposedly he went to Dublin and snuck into London from there. That was April 9th. A couple of weeks later in Miami Lenny walked off stage at the oddly named LeB Buffet Bistro on the 79th street causeway. The police chief of North Bay Village showed up with a sergeant ready to arrest him if he said anything dirty. A terrible review by Herb Kelly in the Miami News brought negative attention. "A Filthy Act Smells Up Classy New Nightclub" said the paper. Lenny was told by police before going up that he should sign a form that his show would be tape recorded for possible prosecution against him, for the alleged obscenity of his act. He was in the second night in a week of shows at the LeB, a late night hot spot on Harbor Isle, on an active chain of industry-residential properties where bartenders and waitresses lived and the after-hours scene was on fire. According to the

Miami Herald, Lenny looked at the cops and left. Business had been good for him there. He celebrated New Year's 1963 at the LeB as a headliner with shows at midnight, 2a.m., and 4a.m. The club was open with continuous music and entertainment from 7p.m. to 7a.m. nightly. You could "Thrill to the most unique dining and dancing and entertainment to be found in Miami Beach" with a complete buffet from 6p.m. to 11p.m. for $4.50 and a Chuck Wagon after 1a.m. for $2.50 per person. The owner of the Le B was Marv Dubbin, and he catered to the type of clientele who were out running around all hours: nightlifers, musicians, actors, entertainers, party girls, and drug dealers, cops, and robbers. Bruce came back and did the late show, and said all the dirty words he wanted. But then on his way out the cops pulled him over and found what a junkie calls his “works.” A hypodermic needle and syringe, glass vials in the glove compartment. They arrested him on felony heroin charges. April 28, 1963 - Comedian Lenny Bruce Arrested - “Saturday night as he hurried to make a nightclub gig with speeding and possession of hypodermic needle and syringe,” said the papers. But he beat the case because the syringe and needle were legally prescribed to him by his Miami Beach doctor for his meth prescription. If it wasn’t for his meth, they might have got him for his heroin. Prescriptions were semantics, and the way that words changed outcomes was a recurring laugh for Lenny. He beat them to the sword with the power of his pen. In fact he would carry a book with him, a scrapbook full of all his prescription labels, notes from doctors, any and all type of evidence he could collect and present at any time to make his case if he had to. That's how good a fast talker he was. Shoulda been a lawyer. Cause all he was doing was telling the truth, but the only thing they ever believed was when he lied. Shit just didn't always work out in the moment some times.

March of 1963, Bruce was found guilty of obscenity in Chicago and was on bond for an arrest in L.A. on charges of suspicion of possessing narcotics. The Chicago conviction got overturned, same for his conviction in NYC, but Lenny was already dead when that happened.

Motherfuckers killed him just for making people laugh.

It was stress after trouble for him in the last couple of years of his life. There was always kicks to be had, but damn if they didn't know how to take the fun out of everything. In November 1963, a news headline hit the United Press wire service and went around the world. "Lenny Bruce Sued By Parents." His 52 year old mother and 34 year old stepfather had filed a $50,000 personal damage claim against him claiming they were injured in his home. "They stumbled over a collection of refuse and lumber, injuring their back, arm, mouth, leg, and foot," said the article. He had asked them to go to his pad and pick up some court transcripts so he could read them on stage at an unnamed club on the Sunset Strip. It was a strange situation. He was four years older than his own stepfather, Tony Viscarra (Later known for playing Junkie in the welfare office in Cheech & Chong's Next Movie). His mom and her husband each wanted $25,000, plus medical care, loss of wages, and attorneys fees.

Maybe that was the beginning of the end. Or maybe the day we're born is. Point being, Lenny Bruce was just trying to have a good time and give a speech like Marcus Aurelius, but he fell out a hotel window in San Francisco and cracked his pelvis, hit his head, and busted his ass while talking to his friend on the sidewalk below.

Leonard Schneider went to war for American Freedom. Hit the high seas for the U.S. Navy during World War II. Sixteen years old and burning on the deck of a massive war hammer floating in a salty universe so deep he felt like he was a centimeter tall and standing on a needle. All that open ocean with its endless pulling tides and rocking waves in 360 degrees of perfect empty everything. Empty like his liquor cup, and empty like his meth syringe. But now he was on stage, half way to Bimini, and laughing about it. Laughing about everything like it was 1963 again.

GEORGE KIRBY

What did the mimic say to the impressionist?

George Kirby had more than 200 voices in his head and nobody could figure out how he made them all talk. He had big eyes the better to see you with, and a hippo jaw that could crack a whole roast chicken easy. He soaked people up through his pores and he had the uncanny ability to sound, move, and act like anybody, man, woman, or child.

He was a World War II Purple Heart decorated veteran who told Miami News reporter Herb Kelly that he was a subject in early LSD medical experiments. Which could explain his heroic level of ability.

There he was. 1957. Surfcomber Hotel. Miami Beach. Doing comedy for Cab Calloway's Cotton Club Revue, reportedly the first all-black show on the beach, with a cast of 50. Big production. Swinging. Dancing. Comedy. Orchestra. All white crowd full of money. The cotton.

Miami Herald. January 7. Jack Kofoed: "Amazing impressionist George Kirby in the Cotton Club Revue."

It was a two week stand to a packed house. All shows sold out. George Kirby was partying. Having a good time doing what he did best, and then doing what came best after. Sparking two fat joints of Jamaican high grade kush fresh off the banana boat, when a real buzz kill showed up, man. Federal agents.

February 22, 1957.

9 Caught In Dope Roundup
Heroin Seized; Marijuana, Too.

By Ronald York. Herald Staff Writer

"A roundup of Miami dope peddlers was launched by federal narcotics agents. Eight suspected salesmen and a ninth man charged with possession. Caught up in the net was George Kirby, 33, of Chicago, working at Miami Beach, charged with possession of two marijuana cigarettes."

Damn. It was an undercover bust starting at 2a.m. The Miami Times reported that a, "Negro FBI agent," working a five week sting infiltrated a small-time drug network through controlled buys. Kirby was in the wrong place at the wrong time, buying weed in Liberty City, roughly Nw 40th St to Nw 79 st between the racist wall and Unity Blvd.

He was already shooting heroin. Apparently his young white wife Sarah Kirby turned him out in Los Angeles years prior and he liked the taste. But what he got arrested with was just a couple sticks of reefer. Marijuana cigarettes. And they gave him $5,000 bond just for that. The 1950's were a bad time for any American to get caught with some weed, let alone a black guy in the south. But six of the other eight people caught in the bust were dealing what the Miami Herald called "Grains of heroin," sold via small capsules in quantities of $2.50 per grain. Some of those two dollar deals would result in ten year mandatory sentences. There was a guy named "Wahoo," and a lady who was the mother of four children who got arrested in the same bust. Everyone but George got $10k bond. Maybe they had great lawyers and got away with it. Anything's possible. George Kirby pulled the comedian's gambit and scored probation. Some people say that standup comics are sociopaths. Charming narcissistic manipulators keenly tuned to human energies. Able to bend the world to their whims via laugh-dopamine, body language, facial expressions, tone, voice, demeanor, cadence, and word choice in a symphony of communicative instruments for the age old fart of confidence. Gotcha. George Kirby saw action as a Combat Engineer for the U.S. Army in Europe and the Philippines for

WWII. He served three years and got to punch a first sergeant in the nose for promoting him. He didn't want the responsibility. He said he wouldn't trade it for the world, but what he really loved was serving big laughs in one of the most popular clubs on the beach, working with Cab Calloway. He'd performed in Miami as early as I could find was 1952, with jazz virtuosos Sarah Vaughn and Stan Kenton in a double header at Dinner Key and Miami Beach Auditoriums. Kirby had toured with red hot mama Sophie Tucker. Performed at Alan Gale's and with Count Basie. Featured in the Miami Herald, the Miami News, the Miami Times. Ten days before his arrest, he was a performer on a Night Of Stars for the Miami Beach Police and Firemen's Benefit at the Dog Track. Two days after he got arrested, he was on a Big Benefit Show For Child Welfare sponsored by the American Legion at Dade County Auditorium. The week after he got arrested, a lamp supposedly got knocked over and set a chair on fire at his room in the Sir John Hotel. Nobody was hurt. Hotel chair fires are typical of dope cooking or nodding off with a lit cigarette. He headlined Vegas, performed on Sullivan. Anybody who had a tv that year saw him on it. His impressions included John Wayne, Frank Sinatra, Ella Fitzgerald, Pearl Bailey, Bill Cosby, Desi Arnaz. Black. White. Cuban. Anybody. Everybody. The judge, the cops, the jury, and the executioner would all recognize him. He was a two hundred forty five pound big man who could make a hundred twenty pound white girl sing through him like a songbird. He once did helicopter sound effects on stage at a veterans function and triggered a guy's PTSD so bad he had a breakdown. It was less like he imitated, more like he became the embodied ridicule through a force field of dissonance between the incongruous form in control of the unexpected output. Hilarious. Kirby did some jail time in a cell on the 23rd floor of the old Dade County Courthouse, but there was a darker confinement he was already trapped in from the inside. The prison of addiction. According to show promos in the newspapers, in 1958, after his arrest, Kirby went right back into Miami comedy, holding down steady work at the Thunderbird Motel in North Miami Beach (the same route as Sammy Shore and Rip Taylor), at the Rocking MB (a year before Flip Wilson), and even for an extended run at the Red Carpet on 16th and Alton, open til 5a.m., with controversial Ray Bourbon, who went to jail for talking about his gay experiences, then became female and even the court didn't know which jail to put him in. Came out and said he wanted to build a jail in his back yard cause that's where the guys were. Kirby needed the work for money to score dope. His own world war too, a never-ending battle between King Heroin and Lady Vein. And there he was, a joker, alive and on probation, but he couldn't stay clean. He worked nights. His best friends were criminals. The streets of Miami were full of the big heavy loads of Golden Triangle Heroin packed in bricks from the Cuban Mafia in Havana. Plus, there was a prescription for everything for the right price. He could smoke it. He could sniff it. He could best of all slam it intravenous back when three piece suits were popular and nobody saw his bare arms anyway. Squirt blood on some hotel room wall, lay on the bed and nod out. Kirby couldn't stop shooting. Hated that he loved it. Knew it was destroying him in a suicidal zyklon nightmare. But the poison was inside him and he didn't want to stop. Even with the cracking, festered flesh wounds, busted blood vessels, staph, bacteria, blown out shot spots, an unsupportable habit fit for a man with unlimited money (he didn't have) enough for his insatiable appetites. The hypodermic cobra's bite had just about killed him. Cause he was hooked after that old war injury like everybody else. The injury to his psyche. All those voices in his head that never stopped yammering. All that combat. He lost hope, let alone motivation. Almost lost his life. So he walked into a U.S. Post Office somewhere in Miami, close to the Carver Hotel in Overtown, and requested a U.S. Marshal, and he turned himself in as a drug addict. And the Marshals gave him a free one-way ticket and an armed escort to the U.S. Public Health Hospital in Lexington, Kentucky, and he kicked heroin cold turkey in the facility's well known Narco treatment program. And at the exact time that he was there, the CIA were conducting LSD experiments at that very same compound. Through Dr. Harris Isbell via the Office of Naval Research in a wide ranging $25 million program by the CIA to study mind control through LSD. And they were recruiting dope sick prisoners, bribing them with opiates in some cases, into a program called Project Bluebird / Artichoke. Sounds made up, but it's not a joke. And they had been doing it there the whole decade, in quantifiably heavy double, and triple doses of Sandoz Laboratories fresh pharmaceutical LSD-25 from Switzerland. So it was known in the heroin underground that all kinds of wacky drug experiments were looking for volunteers in Kentucky, and there was a mostly black male drug treatment program fast tracking entry for all interested parties. Gallons of toxic mustard oozed with rusty opiated sweat that poured out of him in a pneumonic walking death as he detoxed from cocaine, meth, heroin, barbiturates. He crumpled to the floor in a hell of his own making. Metal bed. Bucket. Soul wrenching exorcism via psycho-physiological torture.

Icicles of fire and barb wire hook cells ripped through every artery, vein, and capillary in his mainframe; as oceans of bile erupted from the volcanoes of his thousand degree psychosis, and total-body nerve ending. So much pain and darkness. Then finally, a couple years later, light. When people wrote articles about him, such as in the Nevada State Journal, Kirby described this period as a, "Temporary retirement due to illness." He had heavy problems on the way, but Kirby never glamorized drugs. He actively campaigned against them and always mentored anyone he thought needed to hear about the perils of narcotics. Years later he wrote the dramatic monologue King Heroin, and James Brown recorded it as a song. Unfortunately in 1977, twenty years after getting arrested in Miami, he was set up in a Las Vegas drug sting and busted for selling a pound of heroin for $26,000 to an undercover cop. From two sticks to a whole brick. And then they found his cocaine. Damn. Once again, a months-long set-up caught him in a dragnet. Kirby bragging he was walking loads onto airplanes from Miami to Vegas using his fame to skip the search. Air travel was different at the time. More like riding a public bus through the air. You could still smoke on planes. Yeah, it was easier. If he hadn't sold to a cop, he could've kept right on doing it. His girlfriend's family was connected, he said. I think her street name was Mary Christmas if I'm not mistaken. The dope was pure. He was sentenced to twenty years in federal prison. Twenty. But once again, the comedian overcame. Nobody quite knows what was said or done, or how he did it, but George Kirby got out in three and a half years and went right back to standup comedy.

TONITE ONLY!
CLIMAX CLUB
12001 N.W. 27 AVE.
WILDMAN STEVE BAND & REVUE
RATED XXXX INFORMATION
CALL 688-8481

ISLAND CLUB — 1000 N.E. 2ND AVE.

PRESENTS
THE WILDMAN
STEVE

FEATURING A CAST OF 20

★ QUIVETTES
★ BOBBY JONES
★ BELL BROS.
• GEORGE PATTERSON DANCERS
• FRANK WILLIAMS AND THE ROCKETES

TONIGHT
SAT. — SUN.!

2 SHOWS NIGHTLY
FOR RES. CALL 373-3488

1 st SHOW 11:30

EVERY MONDAY IS TALENT NIGHT. SHOWTIME IS EVERY WED., SAT., SUN.
NEXT WEEK IS OTIS REDDING.

CLYDE KILLEN'S ISLAND CLUB

Presents

HANK BALLARD AND THE MIDNIGHTERS

SATURDAY
MARCH 13

WILDMAN
STEVE
M.C.

SUNDAY
MARCH 14

ORIGINATOR
OF THE
TWIST

2 Shows Nightly • 9:30 and 1:30

10 St. and N.W. 2nd Ave. • FR 3-3488 • Park Free

MIAMI NEW!

CLIMAX NIGHT CLUB

MEMORIAL HOLIDAY
WEEKEND SHOW

12007 N.W. 27th AVE.

FRI.-SAT.-SUN.
MAY 27th-28th-29th

WILDMAN STEVE

COMEDY STAR RATED XXXX

PLUS

RONNIE KEATON

LA FRENCHIE (MIAMI 1st BLACK TRANSEXUAL)

BRAND NEW DISCO BAND

11 P.M. TILL 5:00 A.M. — ADM. $3.00

WILDMAN STEVE

Wildman Steve was wild, man. He was the first Black radio DJ in Boston, on station W-I-L-D, but he started too many revolutions to stay living in New England.

He started out innocent enough. In 1956, Steve Gallon Jr. was a disc jockey for high school dances in Hartford, Connecticut. He also hosted parties in front of a movie screen, as an emcee before the films started at Drive In theaters.

But then in 1957, he was fined $200 for violating state liquor laws. He'd been charged with "Breach of peace and vilifying an officer." According to the Naugatuck Daily News, a Vice Squad Officer named Joseph Guilfoyle busted Wildman Steve for sitting in back of his own restaurant, The Sportsman's Club, where the Brass City DJ was drinking liquor with two ladies past 1a.m. Connecticut blue laws could suck a dick. Must be the guy was some kind of dick sucker. But if that porky pig would have just waited, Steve would have gave it to him right in the rectum. No time for all that though. Thankfully, his charges were dropped.

In 1958, he was still doing small shows in Bridgeport. In 1959, he was on the radio. In 1960, he shared a stage with Redd Foxx. Then Slappy White, Flip Wilson, and Pigmeat Markham, the guy who encouraged him with the axiom of irony: "Steve, you should really take comedy seriously."

As it happened, life was gonna make the decision for him. In September 1962, Wildman inadvertently set off a rock-n-roll riot at Boston Arena when he had to tell an angry crowd that Etta James wasn't showing up and, "2000 rioters battled nearly 100 police" on St. Botolph street, according to the Boston Globe. As the audience lined up for refunds, they started pushing and shoving, you know how Boston is, next thing you know, they got nine paddy-wagons, twenty seven cop cars, tactical shotties, traffic re-routes, and reinforcements. Exactly a year later in September 1963, four people got shot at a show that Wildman Steve was promoting and hosting, a teen dance at, once again, Boston Arena, starring Jackie Wilson. There was a fight on the dancefloor. Someone pulled a pistol and fired six shots. Three boys and a girl suffered bullet wounds. 1,400 youths ran out of Boston Arena fighting. Kids were running across the tops of cars, which were bumper to bumper in melee traffic; throwing rocks and bottles at cops; pulling drivers from their cars and beating them in the streets. Typical Boston. Just another rock 'n' roll riot. Nobody even got arrested. "Negro youth dances with white girl. Fight breaks out," said the papers. Outside of the fighting, another extreme that happened was the crowd got so excited that a group of girls pushed Jackie Wilson to the ground and ripped his clothes off.

Next thing you know Wildman Steve's not on the radio no more, and he's working some little backwood club with too many rules, and then the next time I can find him is in February, 1964, at the all new Hampton House Club in Miami. Wildman Steve presented his Carnival of Stars with R&B rockin' roller and famous comedy lover and Queen of R&B, Ruth Brown ("Time After Time") and a jazz quartet. 1965, at the Mr. James Club, where Flip Wilson worked out, Steve got his own weekly show called Wildman Wednesdays. Bennie Latimore was working there playing the keys, and Little Esther sang her heart out. Hot location. Way better than Connecticut. Open from 12 in the afternoon to 5a.m. with continuous dancing and entertainment! Most beautiful women in the world. And lots of em'. And if he ever hadda go to jail, the guys were good looking too. Wildman Steve was home.

That year, he had a show in Ft. Lauderdale at Porky's. *The* Porky's. He hadda go up there and find some of that good pink meat to eat. Cause Eatin' Ain't Cheatin'. He was doing comedy on a show with Clyde McPhatter from the Drifters, who was starting his solo run. Three shows. One night only. Whoever got to see that got a cool show.

October 1965. Location: Island Club. 1000 NW 2nd Ave. Overtown, Miami, Florida. Site of the former Harlem Square Club where Sam Cooke did his live album. Wild Man Steve's Revue. Big publicity photo. A three night stand with a teenage matinee on Sunday afternoon at a reduced price for the neighborhood kids. Headliner is the hardest working man in show business. James Brown, backed by saxophonist Dizzy Jones, the local favorites Frank Williams and The Rocketeers, and the Continentals. This is Overtown. Malcolm X is dead. The U.S. is in a Vietnam War. Race riots in Watts. The Beatles, Help! Wildman is showboating and show promoting, but he's really not doing headline sets of standup comedy yet. He's a professional MC, promoter, party host. How's that for vertical integration. He's a radio guy, pimping record labels for artists for his parties, LP's for promotions, working the distributors to cut himself deals, and selling boxes of albums backdoor to the store owners he's cool with.

Typical activities. Bringing down La Vern Baker to the James Club with Them Two, Pharaoh and The Cool Ones, Cornbread and The Rocking Five on the day of the Orange Blossom Classic Parade. Free front row tables. Morgan State beat Florida A&M 36 - 7. It was good being the Wildman. Steve Gallon Jr. was born in Monticello, Florida but moved to Connecticut as a little kid and grew up there, so this might have been his first live Orange Blossom Classic parade experience, a street and club party attached to arguably the best college football game of the year, between teams from Historically Black Colleges and Universities. The parade went from Liberty City to Overtown and that was a festival the likes of which have never been seen in Miami since. Big shows followed. With Lloyd Price or Johnny Nash at the Island Club. Or hosting a revue at the Kandy Bar. The show flier said, "The only go-go girl revue in the Palm Beaches." He worked in Pompano Beach, and in Cocoa Beach with Roy Hamilton. By 1966 he was on WMBM as a DJ. The station had a broadcast signal originating in Miami Beach, with a substation in the heart of Overtown, with a studio behind the glass of a big street-facing window, so everybody walking the busy neighborhood could see the DJ at work. The hottest R&B station in Florida and a trend setter in the U.S. He would work his hours in the studio, then take off on weekends like comics do. In December of 1966, he MC'd the big Sam and Dave show at Dinner Key Auditorium, where Ray Charles and The Doors played, and the current site of Miami City Hall. Tickets were $3 in advance or $3.50 the day of. Sam & Dave were backed by a ten piece orchestra and were in the heat of "Hold On I'm Coming." 1967, "Soul Man" topped the national charts and Steve opened at The Barn on 79th street, the famous home of a wild and wacky speedfreak named Wayne Cochran, with a foot high white pompadour. There's only one James Brown, but if there was any room for anyone else, Wayne Cochran was the white James Brown. Funny character. Became a preacher. I went to his church and while I was smoking a joint sitting on the trunk of my car in the parking lot of the stripmall plaza he was based out of in Miami Gardens / Carol City, he pulled up in a Cadillac and a brother opened his door and took his jacket off his shoulders. Hilarious. Steve worked The Barn with Harold Melvin and The Blue Notes, and a group called the Dancing Parkettes I'm guessing everyone called them the parakeets. The place was open to 7a.m. if you can believe it, with no admission, no cover, a three drink minimum, and three shows a night. In 1968, Wildman was at the Club Oasis in Tampa with dancers, singers, and soul bands, then jumping up to Connecticut to do the same, for one night only, maybe visiting family. In Virginia, he joined the Jeannie C. Riley "Harper Valley PTA Revue" hitting Roanoke, Atlanta, and Charlotte with seven acts, including Wilson Pickett (Mustang Sally, In The Midnight Hour, Funky Broadway). These big touring package shows were a laugh riot with everybody traveling and hanging out together through every stop, start, and argument, finding each other's nerves, poking and laughing. Welcome to the circuit. He closed out the year back Miami way at the Turf Double Deck Bar on 79th Street and NW 7th Ave, always been a real active block. Wide open on 79, at all times. According to the show poster in the newspaper, Frank Sinatra filmed the Tony Rome bar scene there. 1969, he ran the Wildman Steve Sophisticated Soul Show at the Apartment Lounge on 175th and Biscayne Boulevard. NMB, short for North Miami Beach, where Sammy Shore used to live. Wildman brought in Latimore, before his big hit and now highly sampled soul classic "Let's Straighten It Out."

Then in 1969, it finally happens. He was back at the Kandy Bar in West Palm Beach. "Wild Man Steve. The most unusual comic in showbiz. Are you 100% shockproofed. Wild Man Steve, sophisticated "shock" comedian. Open til 5a.m., lucky ticket, door prizes, and dancing nightly." It's the first time I find the word comedian next to his name. 1970, guy wouldn't stop working. There he was in York, Pennsylvania with Isaac Hayes. There he was at the Soul City in Ft Lauderdale. In Philly with The O'Jays. In Greensboro, North Carolina with the Plantation Dancers. 1971, Atlantic City with Jackie Wilson for the Easter Sunday show at Club Harlem. After that, off to the real Harlem to perform at The Apollo. The Apollo. The Apollo. Say it eight or nine times cause that's how many times in a row he played it. 1971, back in Tampa, now billed as Wild Man Steve, Raw Records Comedy Star. Show rated XXX. He was solidified to who he was. "A man that tells it just like it is." Now dig this. Steve had a lifelong career doing some form or other of independent shows. That's why even though this is a Miami book it's also an America book. Cause this one guy with nothing but his friends and his voice box and what's an agent, and what's a manager, and what's the mainstream, was crossing over America one club at a time, Johnny comedy seed out there planting laugh trees, and then going back to Miami, and repeating the cycle. There he was at Asbury Park, New Jersey's famous Orchid Lounge with his soul revue. At the Ponderosa in Neeses, South Carolina. Buffalo. Knoxville. Charlotte, North Carolina with his redneck white friend Gene Tracy doing a racial buddy comedy act at Big Daddy's Lounge, featuring

Miyya Lee the Fire Goddess and a five girl topless revue. Tits! Then back to New Jersey for 2 shows nightly.

January 23, 1974. He was back to the Apollo in Harlem, this time with Sylvia Robinson, who had that song "Pillow Talk," and was gonna use those profits to found Sugar Hill Records in a few years. Steve was there with Fatback Band, and his best friend Latimore, who had finally scored a hit with "Stormy Monday," a cover of the old T-Bone Walker blues jam. Then on down to Orangeburg, South Carolina, and Raleigh, North Carolina. You may not expect it either, but these big old southern parties were all mixed, black and white. Crackas and Niggas together laughing at each other and themselves. He spoke about this phenomenon later in life. Black and white together in the south. And all black up north. That's how his audiences demographed regionally. Even in Oakland California, November, 1975. Recording his new album at Ed Howard's Place. That's the way it went for years and years.

Memorial weekend 1977, he performed at the Climax Club with a famous local character, "La Frenchie, Miami's first black transexual."

Then he got into movies. Films. Cinema. In 1977, he co-starred with his old friend Rudy

Ray Moore in *Petey Wheatstraw The Devil's Son In Law*. A great movie, that still holds up. 1978 saw the release of, *Ain't That Just Like A Honkey*, with Wildman Steve in the starring role. In 1978, he starred in *The $6,000 Nigger*, a parody of the 6 Million Dollar Man also known as *Super Soul Brother*. The only "blaxploitation" film shot in Miami also features Latimore, solid cinematography, and a great look at 1970s Miami if you pay attention to the scene locations. It was not a main-run feature at the big theater chains, but it did play nationally at a cool number of drive-ins. Controversial title, but a solid watchable flick.

That was some interesting points in the life of Steven Gallon, Jr. Korean War Veteran of the U.S. Navy, and a Golden Gloves Middleweight Champion boxer. He was on the first ever Def Comedy Jam. His first albums outsold Richard Pryor. When he retired, he helped broke people find jobs. He died in 2004 at 78 years old in Miami, Florida with a wife, eight kids, thirteen grandkids, and eight great grandkids. He kept close with the people he cared for and he stayed Wildman all the way.

APPEARING NIGHTLY

IRV "KOKIE" KOLKER who has introduced to MIAMI BEACH SAMMY DAVIS JR. — SALLY BLAIR — DUKE HAZLETT and BARBARA McNAIR . . . now proudly presents the NEW and FABULOUS GREAT STAR—

MISS PEARL WILLIAMS

"THE SAUCY GIRL" Who has sold over

1,000,000 Albums

Broke all records at the CASTAWAYS HOTEL, LAS VEGAS—24 Weeks

CHUCK BARI, Miami Beach's newest singing sensation, and a complete REVUE

SHOWTIMES 9:30 - 12:15 - 2:15

DOWNSTAIRS ROOM entrance on ground floor THE SEVILLE HOTEL

29th St. and Collins Ave. . . Reservations JE 2-1471

ONLY 14 MORE NIGHTS TO SEE PEARL

PEARL WILLIAMS OPENS ON SAT. NIGHT, DEC. 19th AT PLACE PIGALLE, M.B.

THE SPICY GAL WHO SHOCKED LAS VEGAS

PAULY DASH
COMEDY M.C.

PSYCHEDELIC SENSATION
"MISS ADDIE"

NO ADMISSION NO COVER
CONTINUOUS SHOW 9 P.M. TO 5 P.M.
ALL CREDIT CARDS HONORED

THIS IS BURLESQUE
SATAN'S ANGEL
"THE DEVIL'S MISTRESS"

AND HER ALL GIRL REVUE
42"-25"-36"

THE FREEMAN SISTERS
"WITH THEIR SUPREME VOCAL STYLINGS FROM LAS VEGAS"

Place Pigalle

COLLINS at 22nd AVE. M.B. — 558-0055, 538-0042

PEARL WILLIAMS

Pearl Williams was a pretty little legal secretary from the Lower East Side of Manhattan who wanted to be a New York State Supreme Court Judge and was 15 credits shy of an NYU law degree, who found herself twenty five years later on stage at 5a.m. at the Place Pigalle on Miami Beach with two big arches drawn on her forehead singing about getting her knish ate from the back to a couple hundred clapping, laughing, drunken fools. It all started when her friend needed a piano player for a club audition way back in nineteen thirty somethin', and a guy named Feet was listening. Feet Edson liked her style, got her a gig with Louie Prima, and then at a clip joint, a bust-down, a bar that used broads and music to lure in suckers and then overcharged em' for drinks. They had muscle on hand for whoever didn't wanna pay. They all paid. She started bringing home hundreds of bucks and her mom thought she was a whore in Chicago. But the only ivories she was tickling were her piano keys. She played straight up club-piano, no jokes, for eighteen years and then snapped one night when a heckler said "Show your tits bitch!" Pearl told him, "Fuck off you no dick having little faggot, you wouldn't know what to do with a pair of tits if you were the farmer's wife!" (or something along those lines). The whole club broke up and that's how she started comedy. Sometime in the mid-sixties she moved to Miami Beach, walked up to Harry Ridge, the owner of the Place Pigalle, and said, "Hey, it's me, Pearl Williams. I start tomorrow." And she did. Big funny fat lady in a cherry red zipper front dress, looking like a fire hydrant. She had more makeup than a clown, but you know what, she had a nice face but she could be so mean, which made her pretty and ugly at the same time. Pretty ugly. People love that combo. The crowd saw her like family. Damn was she quick. A real wit. Owned the stage like a union boss. Big voice. Lotta singing. Lotta Hovva Naggilla. Pearl Williams started performing in Miami in 1946 and never stopped till she pushed it to the illogical extreme when she retired from the Place Pigalle in 1984, the last of the old Miami Beach nightclubs. She worked there from 1966 with a lot of the same strippers and audiences year after year, cultivating a mystic status on 23rd and Collins Ave; and the day she hung up her joke shoes, the place went slowly out of business.

Place Pigalle. I don't know how to pronounce it. Pig Alley? Pig Al? Peegal? It's French, but I think its origin is a street corner in Philly where the whores work overtime. Just kidding. It's a famous town-square in a neighborhood of Paris, France, next to a subway stop, surrounded by bars on all sides, where artists liked to party back in the day. There's still a few joints around in the U.S. that carry the name.

The Place Pigalle at 215 22nd St, across from the Miami Beach Public Library, was an adult entertainment venue, strip joint, comedy club, and old style showroom with a full bar, restaurant, and exotic dancers. Tits and ass, joke slingers, and good times. Mostly good times. There was that one berserk Korean kid who bought a stripper some drinks, left angry, came back at three in the morning jumping out of a taxi with guns in each hand blasting. He killed a Canadian baritone opera singer named Tony D'Arcy, shot the doorman David Goodman in the legs, got rushed by dancer Sharon Sutton, very brave, who was a topless g-string comedian with an upside-down can-can act. He shot her in the gut and the pelvis and she ended up losing a leg in the hospital. The dishwasher Saly "Whitey" Hoffner threw a bongo drum at the shooter like he was a gorilla tossing a barrel over his head and knocked a gun out of his hand, then MC Earl Van tackled him, and Goodman, the doorman with the bullets in his legs used Sweet Richard's machete from his act to whack that motherfucker in the head while the cops showed up, and maybe when they had him cuffed too. That was a dark day. But the people knew how the owner Harry Ridge let Veterans drink free, bussed over hospital floors full of wounded soldiers to show them a good time, and was known to be a stand up guy in general. Lee Sohn was a Korean guy (not the shooter) who sang American standards there for decades to great acclaim. Tee Tee Red, Baby Doll, Sherry Champagne, Blaze Starr, Tempest Storm, Dixie Evans, they all danced at the Pigalle. There were multiple employees who worked there for the full thirty year run of the club. Including the strippers. Every year their costumes fit different. From g strings to geeeee strings as the fabric stretched. But the place printed money. Fans came in from around the world, looking for that Pearl Williams style of dirty Yiddish New York American yappin' laughing insult rappin' Eastern European Miami Beach Jewish comedy. Jews, and Irish Catholics, and Italians, Cubans in the mix, oh the conference parties full of drunken white Shriners looking for a good time, the bronze contingent, the ebony express, Latins in banana boats, the Rhumba Casino around the corner, a real good cross section of all society, the crowds were as funny to look at as the comics, aged too young to 98 from everywhere and anywhere. Partyin'. There was a whole scene of dirty talking lady Jewish comedians at the time but Pearl Williams really had her own thing with Sophie Tucker and Belle Barth. Pearl was always helping out young comics and singers, with money or time or connections. She had a real particular laugh, a good funny one, which is one of the comic tricks, to have a good laugh, not a fake one, a good one. On stage. She laughed kinda lazy and amused, like a cat on cat nip. Real distinct. You can hear it in the crowd on one of Flip Wilson's records in New York. She was a party-record famous comedian too, sold millions, starting on the same label around the same time as Belle Barth, and her work was advertised in trade pubs and club show posters as "Over 1,000,000 Sold!" then, "Over 3,000,000 million sold." Pearl was an earner, and a worker from the Lower East Side of NYC. The daughter of Austrian or Russian Jew immigrants depending who you asked. She graduated Seward Park High School and was a take-no-shit character. When she started playing piano, she was a lawyer's secretary making eighteen bucks a week. She made a hundred fifty bucks her first week in the clubs and dropped out of school. Broadway talent scout Feet Edson got her on a show with Jackie Gleason and Joe Frisco. Frank Sinatra told her to go for it. From there it was no looking back. Feet was old friends of Joe E. Lewis and Sophie Tucker. They helped her too. Pearl's first Miami show was in 1946 at Jack Dempsey's club in the Vanderbilt Hotel, which later became the Coronet where Belle had her pub. Jack Dempsey the fighter had a place too. Everything was one offs, or one week stands, or two weeks held over. There were one-nighters, and seasons, and capitals, and gangsters, and the stakes were high. In 1954, Pearl performed at a hotel on 7th street and Dade Boulevard with a host named Little Yankel. In 1955, good old Uncle Miltie Sackett discovered her and had her in the Vendome on 43rd and Collins. In 1956, she put in time with B.S. Pully, at the Vanity Fair Lounge at 1601 79th St., with dancing till 7a.m. in Miami's, "Newest late night spot," with shows at 3a.m. Talk about complete dinners. Free comedy, no cover, no minimum, prime New York cut sirloin steak or whole broiled pompano fish for $3.95. Who the hell broils a pompano? That's a grill fish!

Pearl was married twice, and her second husband Joe Kant had been the maitre d at the Latin Quarter on Palm Island for fourteen years. Good old Joe, she loved, but he passed away from cancer in 1957.

In 1961, she had her After Hours records label debut, "A Trip Around The World Is Not Cruise," (around-the-world being a euphemism for sexual intercourse, which is a technical term for fuckin). This was a hit. Sounds like it was recorded in New York. I don't know. She was big in Montreal and

Chicago too. But I think it's NYC. Clean audio, funny crowd, raucous show.

Later, she did a couple albums with Laff Records that were recorded in Miami Beach, at The Cabaret on 23rd street off Collins Ave, which in 1968 called itself, "The newest most beautiful niteclub in Miami Beach." The proprietor was Irv "Kokie" Kolker, a club promoter in Miami Beach and Atlantic City who had South Florida connections with The Surfcomber, Copa City, Vanity Fair, Embers, and The Seville. The two albums Pearl recorded at The Cabaret are, "You'll Never Remember It, Write It Down!" and "Bagels And Lox." Funny shit. Classic even. Give them a listen. I dare you. She's a female Rickles. If you ever saw his Vegas show in life or on youtube, it's a traditional borscht belt style that combines written material, crowd work, instrumental backing, and some jewish power anthems to round out the show. Everybody knows that John Wayne had a picture of Hitler up in his cowboy hat, but in 1970, John Wayne Jr. dropped in on Pearl Williams at the Pigalle. It made the newspaper. She was long friends with the whole family. In 1971, she celebrated 33 years in the business, she told Ken Heinrich from the Miami News, "The two stars dearest to me were Belle Barth and Sophie Tucker." She got to hang out with them on the beach. Sophie,

Belle, and Pearl. Woulda been a great podcast. If only they were obsessed with recording equipment as Lenny Bruce. He used to carry a briefcase around with a hidden recorder in it, maybe he got some good audio on them.

In 1978, Pearl was at Jefferson's cosmetic counter on North Miami Beach Boulevard, when she turned her head to talk to a clerk, and someone stole the purse she left on the counter with $500 cash in it.

In 1984, she announced her retirement from the Place Pigalle. The last of the old school MB nightclubs. The dawn of the Marielito era of brash and open crime and scarface level violence over cocaine, weed, and paranoid emotions.

For six months she relaxed, knitted, crocheted, spent hours in the studio with her friend Peppy Fields on her AM radio talk-show, the original podcast. She liked a good nap, the lazy days. But without Pearl, the old Pigalle fell apart. People stopped coming. Owner Harry Ridge renamed it the Go Go 22 and slapped on a new paint job that nobody cared for. He called Pearl. Begged. Cajoled. Wept. "Please, Pearl," he said "Can't you do one more season for me, baby?"

...

..

“Harry, you fucking fuck, for you, I’ll do it.”

And she did.

(clockwise) Pearl Williams, Sammy Shore, George Kirby, H.S. Gump - publicity photos

HELD OVER!

The Hollywood Sensation

B. S. PULLY

ASSISTED BY

H. S. GUMP

• • PLUS • •

BALLARD & RAE

COMEDY CAPERS

IRIS KARYL • BILLY LOWE

DANCE STYLIST • SINGING EMCEE

TWO ORCHESTRAS — CONTINUOUS DANCING

CHINESE AND AMERICAN CUISINE

BY THE ORIGINAL FU MANCHU

SHOWS 11-2-4

The PADDOCK CLUB

For RESERVATIONS 5-4071

Washington Ave. at 7th St.

B.S. PULLY

B.S. Pully always had dice in his pocket, laughter in his blood, a razor in his step, a gleam in his eye, a joke in his heart, and a fist for the face of anyone who wanted to find out.

He was a walking, talking, human laugh machine. One of those everything he says is funny New York gangster guys that only makes it to showbiz every 70 years or so. An underdog.

Kliph Nesteroff's book says that B.S. Pully had a cigar box with a hole cut in it that he would do a dick-in-a cigar-box to strippers just for fun in the clubs they worked together. He was on Broadway's biggest musical for fucks sakes, but his true personality got to shine in the after hours of the types of places that made him who he was.

He was Big Jules the crapshooter who never missed in the musical Guys and Dolls. And the man with over thirty film credits in Hollywood.

And he was B.S. Pully the underground strip club comic so dirty that half of Connecticut law enforcement, plus the FBI, and the Assistant U.S. Attorney were allied against him. Unfortunately for them, it's impossible to violate community standards if the whole community loves you.

Anyway, they didn't hurt Pully. They arrested nine people who were selling a product he probably wouldn't get paid on anyway, the record business being what it is, and the audio mix of his album is rough listening, on the original and the bootleg of the bootleg.

Ups and downs followed Pully like dogs chase rabbits. He was always at the track. According to him, always losing. That was his running joke to the newspapers. The inveterate gambler, always on the come-up from a heartbreaking loss. Constantly borrowing from friends to try to win it back. Having to pay it all back every time he won. Whenever he got a movie role, he'd use the money to pay off all his bad bets from the last year. He used to joke about it. But in Guys and Dolls he shot craps and never lost, and maybe that was closer to the truth. How he became Big Jules in the musical about gangsters and broads from a story by Damon Runyon is that he went to the tryouts for the show with his comic friend Gene Baylos cause it was action. Pully had a big bark of a voice. New York gravel. Every time he exhaled, it let off smoke like a bus engine. The director George S. Kaufman heard him speak and called him over. "Pully, you think you could play a crapshooter?" B.S. pulled a pair of dice from his pocket.

Miami News
January 1951
by Earl Wilson

B.S. Pully Gets Role As Crapshooter - But He's Had 30 Years Practice. "I been a hustler, I been a cab driver, I been in jail. But I always knew dat I'd be good on stage."

He had dozens of acting roles in films from 1944 - 1970 including A Tree Grows In Brooklyn, Greenwich Village, Hole In The Head, Lady In Cement, and a handful with leggy pinup model Betty Grable.

B.S. Pully was born May 14, 1910 in Newark, New Jersey. He died January 6, 1972 in Philadelphia, Pennsylvania.

He got married in Miami Beach. Had a kid in Miami Beach. Took his kid fishing and caught a big sailfish off Miami Beach. And he got to enjoy the 1940s there as its most highly regarded dirty comic. A sort of joker to the king of the nightlife, Joe E. Lewis, one of his great friends, who always had some cash for his pal at the track.

The first time I can find him in the Miami area is January 1946, but for all I know he used to be here all his life. Whatever. WWII was over, and Americans were drinking off the shadows of the atom bomb. Spending on entertainment was up, and going upper. B.S. Pully at the Paddock Club, where Honey Harlow danced a few years later, turned that whole joint's fortunes around. According to the Miami News, "The place seemed to have a jinx on it. B.S. Pully and his able assistant H.S. Gump came on the scene. Now, the Paddock is a madhouse, operating at capacity for seven straight nights, says operator Harry Friedlander." They had a celebrity breakfast show at 4a.m. with authentic Chinese and American cuisine by Chef Fu Manchu. "A laugh a second." 7th street and Washington Ave. Dance til 6a.m.

H.S. Gump was B.S. Pully's comic foil, the so-called, "Gnomeish" (short king) guy he worked with at all the best and worst places in the country for years and years. Their names stood for Bull Shit Pully and Horse Shit Gump. They grew up together, "He stopped growing," joked Pully, in the Bronx. They met in the first grade, where they'd tell each other's teachers their parents were calling to cut class, and by second grade they dropped out of school altogether to hustle full time.

January 1947, "Hollywood wants him. The parole board is looking for him. The landlady needs him. But unfortunately we got him. B.S. Pully assisted by H.S. Gump. 3 shows nitely. Breakfast show at 3:30a.m. Kitty Davis Theater. 1610 Alton Road. Miami Beach." As you can read, he had an established character in the area.

In 1947, Pully got married to Hope Carter on Allison Island in north beach, real posh like. They had a kid called Steve. Steven Alan Lerman. Today he's a lawyer out in LA and he was Rodney King's lawyer during the LA Riots.

Pully and Hope were living in the Blackstone Hotel and he could be found cracking em' up at the Blackstone Hotel for its Laff Riot of '47.

He kept working the beach. Harder than ever, with more mouths to feed. There he was at Don Richard's Famous Door. Greatest laff show on the beach. 223 twenty third street. Again, right in that little 20 to 23rd street off Collins Ave. In the 40s, the Rumba Casino had a Liberty Ave entrance. Hot area.

H.S. Gump got married in 1947, to Mary Gray, right there on the stage of the Paddock Club. B.S. Pully was his best man.

That same year, Pully was the opening act at the Albion Hotel on Lincoln Road and James Ave. Still there today. Place next door ended up being one of the early headquarters of the Bang Bus porn video company. I used to work there around 2005.

B.S. Pully and H.S. Gump liked doing comedy in anything-goes strip clubs where they could run their favorite gags and bits. They were funnier than a lot of the comics doing showrooms, and theaters, and fancy nightclubs in the area. The A rooms were boring, stuffy, behavior based, more about the crystal chandelier than the jokes. Humorless places where dicks got hard and pussies wet for the money in the room. Pully and Gump had to be funny enough to entertain more than 30 naked ladies. And be more entertaining than 30 naked ladies too! An impossible feat that they never stopped trying to pull off. The clubs were the optimal creative outlet for a true bullshit artist and his favored style of humor.

The comic extremes encapsulated his incongruous nature as dick joke comedian and Hollywood star.

Here's what else you gotta know about Pully in Miami:

In 1950, he got his own B.S. Pully Pump Room at the WM Penn Hotel on 7th street and Washington. He was working with his hilariously named cohort Shirley The Hawk, New-Nose Nora, Barry Mack, and good old Horse Shit Gump.

Pully lived at some point with his family at 7524 Mutiny Ave. on Treasure Island, four blocks south of the 79th street causeway. The after-hours zone.

In August 1947, he got sued by a lady and her mother for allegedly cussing them out when they told him not to make her baby laugh. The baby was in a carriage on Washington Ave, on a bright, sunny, beautiful Miami Beach day.

What was he doing trying to make a random baby laugh? He's a comic that's what. It was his job, his swore bound duty to make strangers crack up. Case went to court, made the papers, everything. Hilarious.

"Mrs. Dora Keller contends the comedian became orally abusive when she and her daughter asked him not to play with the four-month-old baby lying in a carriage in front of 735 Washington Ave."

Pully did the right thing. Deny, deny, denied the charges of using profane language in front of Mrs. Keller and her daughter. Ultimately, the judge delayed a trial until the lady could find witnesses, and I think nothing ever came of it.

Another situation that Pully had on Miami Beach is when he got sued over an ice skater in 1946. Her name was Sonja Henie, from Norway. And Sonja Henie is still the winningest World Title and Olympic Champion in female figure skating history. She was a 1930s Hollywood starlet. There was an altercation that ensued between B.S. Pully and Sonja Heine's chauffeur, George Scharf, down there on the strip somewhere, and George got his ass beat by Pully and hospitalized. National gossip columnist Dorothy Kilgallen dropped a rumor that Pully offered Scharf ten thousand bucks to settle out of court. Pully pulled no punches. The Miami Herald reported that he was "fined $25 and costs and given a suspended five-day jail sentence for assaulting the cab driver." He probably deserved it.

In 1955, Pully was at the Five O'Clock Club, holding forth in an intimate Parisian revue, called Peepholes Of Paris. There were fifteen named strippers on the advertisement, such as Snooky DeWitt, Jeanne Delta, and Honey

Harlow, the famous Hot Honey Harlow who you can see in a movie she starred in with Lenny Bruce called Dance Hall Racket.

In January 1957, Sam Goldwyn, the G from MGM, gave Pully a thousand dollar bill for making him laugh at a party.

Later that year, B.S. Pully was headlining at the Place Pigalle, "The only authentic French follies revue in North America!" He worked with Rhonda The Jungle Siren, and Dixie Evans, "Dead ringer for Marilyn Monroe." Continuous shows to 5a.m. No cover. 30 beautiful, exciting girls.The hottest most shocking showplace in America. Welcome all VFW."

In 1968, Pully threw a birthday party for H.S. Gump. They had been working together for forty years. Best of friends. Frank Sinatra was there, and he officially announced Pully for a role in his new film Lady In Cement. Pully said, great, man, he needed the cash. It was also his 29th anniversary. That's how many years it had been since he stepped up to the cash window at Hialeah Race Track. He was due for a win.

One time when he was arrested for his act, he left the court room saying, "I'm a fugitive from a joke."

LAWANDA PAGE
AUNT ESTHER
•
WILDMAN STEVE
•
BLOW FLY
•
RUDY RAY MOORE
ON TOUR

ACHIEVERS HALL — SAT. OCT. 30th
9320 N.W. 27th Ave. Miami, Fla.
Info. (305) 693-1312   Doors Open 9 P.M.

Thurs. Oct. 28th — Sunset Lounge — West Palm Beach
Fri. Oct. 29th — Down Beat Club — Ft. Lauderdale
Sun. Oct. 31st — 100 West Lounge — Orlando

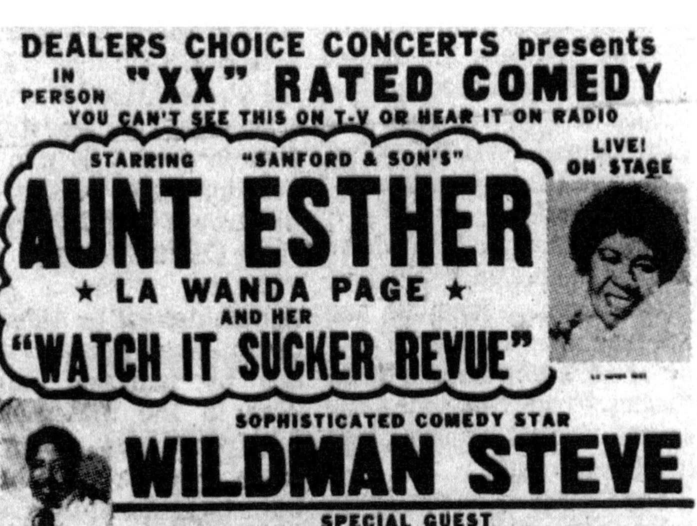

The "Watch It Sucker" Comedy Jam

This Sun. Sept. 6th

Starring "Aunt Esther" LaWanda Page

From The Redd Foxx TV Show

also featuring Wildman Steve

Candy Baby • Simply Marvelous • Wilbert G. & Willie B.

STUDIO 183

2860 N.W. 183rd St. • Sept. 6th 8PM

For Information & Tickets Call

621-7925 or 836-2688

Adv. Adm. $18. At Door $20.

LAWANDA PAGE

La Wanda Page. La Wanda. La Wanda. LAWANDA!

She used to be on every show with the Soul Clowns Of Comedy and they never would put her name on the marquee. Used to drive her damn crazy. But at least Leroy and Skillet were hilarious and that made her even funnier. Lie may not sharpen cheat. But steel does sharpen steel.

In 1971, she came to the Crater Room at The Jetaway on 27th ave and 36th street, about a mile east of Miami International Airport, for a comedy special with M.C. Poison Head, music by Little Beaver's Thunder Lightning & Rain, and entertainment by the Soul Clowns of Comedy: Skillet & Leroy, plus LaWanda "The Queen Of Comedy." There. See. They did put her in the credits. But, in 1972, they came back and they put her name Lawanda, but they didn't call her queen of comedy. In 1973, the flier only said Skillet & Leroy. And in 1974, it was Skillet & Leroy & Cathy. Cathy? That's who they brought. Cathy. A would be replaceable or at least interchangeable role in their versions of classic theater, original skits, time proven characters, and gags. Leroy &

Skillet was like two Pigmeat Markhams on stage at once, talking to each other. Loud. With Cathy in the middle in a bikini doing her job. Consummate entertainers and their records were megasellers as well. But by the 80's, the show was La Wanda's to sell. Sanford and Son had visually solidified her for a national audience. In October 1982 she headlined the Achiever's Hall on 93rd street and NW 27th Ave. 27th Ave is Unity Blvd, an important cultural artery going all the way from Biscayne Bay in Coconut Grove to Loxahatchee Road in Broward County. From what she said in the press, LaWanda loved the hood. You can see her in LA in the streets with the people, showing love, and from reading what she had to say, that was a big part of who she was, not just an image. Working with Wildman Steve in Miami, with him doing the work of booking and promoting and advertising and organizing, they could run an independent production, and perhaps take home more money than if they had gone through traditional channels at higher paid gigs at more prominent venues, with everyone else taking a cut along the way. That's what Latimore described as, "It's not what you make. It's what you take home that counts." Even well into her days of being rich and established as Aunt Esther on Sanford and Son, which ran for six seasons on NBC, Lawanda continued playing Miami hood venues. When Redd Foxx brought her into Sanford and Son, the network hated her and even she thought it could never work. She did explicit material on the LA underground. But Foxx knew her from St. Louis. He believed in her. Helped her practice. And she knocked it outta the park. The show in 1982 at Achiever's Hall featured LaWanda Page, Wildman Steve, the OG dirty rapper Blowfly, and Rudy Ray Moore as Dolemite on one of the longstanding South Florida touring routes from Miami, to Broward, up to Orlando, then back down to West Palm. It seems it was a success because La Wanda came back in December with the same lineup at Andre's Town Club for Christmas weekend 1982. Location: a couple of miles away from Criteria Hit Factory where Michael Jackson and Eric Clapton cut million sellers and Tom Dowd perfected 8-track stereo recording. "You can't see this on tv. You can't hear this on the radio. This is live on stage!" screamed the flier. In 1983, the package was back. Jetaway Lounge. 2724 N.W. 36th St. A $5 show in advance, or $7 at the door. It was a Dealers Choice Concerts presents production, based out of Wildman Steve Enterprises at 1012 NW 74th St, a filming location from the parody blaxploitation movie that he starred in along with his good friend, Blues Hall of Fame singer /songwriter Latimore. Dealers Choice was also the label for the 1980 Wildman Steve album called Is It Good Baby, which attributes all its comedy writing to Vicky Gallon, which, either she was a very funny lady, or Wildman Steve was protecting royalty bearing assets under his wife's performance collecting name. The show was advertised adults-only for mature audiences. "In person XX comedy starring Sanford & Son's Aunt Esther La Wanda Page and her Watch It Sucker Revue with Wildman Steve, Ronnie Keaton, Mel Ford & The Triple X Band."

Before she became Aunt Esther for Redd Foxx on NBC's Sanford and Son, La Wanda was looking like she was going to be making 80-bucks a week as a no-credit sidekick in southern California comedy halls for the rest of her life. While the owners of Laff Records fucked her out of all her royalties like she was the queen of England at a satanic orgy. There she was, one of the top selling comedians in the country and she might not even know it. Everyday people didn't read Billboard, Cashbox, or Record World. Didn't see the full page ads or track the charts. Those were trade papers. She may have had no idea that about 30 independent distributors in all the major markets in the country, mostly big cities, were actively tracking all of her releases, and buying them by the hundreds and sometimes thousands to sell retail in their markets. Comics might have known this was all tied in with the mafia, and the small-time two bit record hustlers of the world, with con artists, and grifters, and drug addicts, and derelicts, and degenerates, and gamblers, and alcoholics, and nymphos, and every shape, size, and nomenclature of loud, rude, and in-your-face bad breath mug in the music business. But they wouldn't know where or how to find them, let alone collect on the arcane system of credit, chargebacks, and promo copies that structured the whole industry. All La Wanda knew was that Redd Foxx used to be a nasty little funny motherfucker when they were kids in St Louis together at the same school (she was two years older), and thanks to Redd Foxx, mama, she was going to be rich and famous and on tv.

LaWanda the freaky comedian who talked about all kinds of sucking and fucking on stage and on record, and played the cleanest old church lady on tv. She wore frumpy clothes, wig, wrinkle makeup, and fooled everybody, starting with Benjamin Franklin, on how to dive face first in her pursey and make her rich. Even after which she stayed living in the same humble abode and taking care of her family.

Hilarious lady with great jokes and she was close with Wildman Steve and his wife Vicky and even used to stay with them for a while at a time down in Miami and really have a ball.

She started out in entertainment as "The Bronze Goddess" doing a fire routine at the Faust Club in East St. Louis. Playing with fire is how she made her money, but every time she did it she got burned. How's that for a Faustian bargain? You can find scantily clad and bikini promo shots of her from her early career and she was real attractive, which is just funny because of the character she got famous for.

La Wanda Page was hilarious. One of the best uncensored comics to ever go pop.

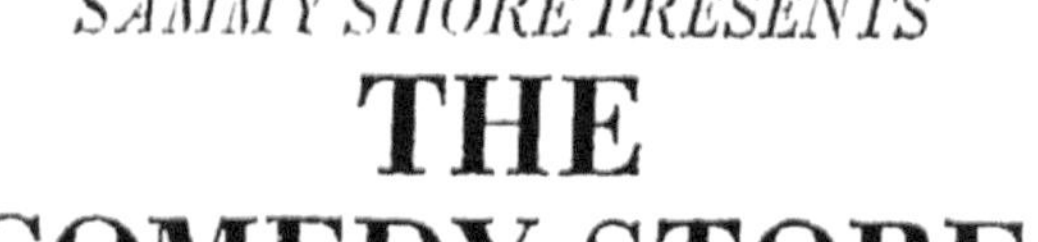
SAMMY SHORE PRESENTS
THE
COMEDY STORE
"Home of America's Top Comedians"
TUESDAY thru SATURDAY
8433 SUNSET STRIP
656-9263
WED. NIGHT FEATURING TOP BLACK COMEDIANS

SAMMY SHORE

From a Florida shore to the Comedy Store. Sammy Shore, nationally touring headliner, and the future founder of the home of Richard Pryor comedy in Hollywood, California, lived with his wife Mitzi and two kids (at the time) Sandy and Scotty, in North Miami Beach at 971 NE 175th Street from around 1957 to 1964. Pauley Shore wasn't born yet. Sammy worked the clubs, the lounges, and the nightclub showrooms as an emcee, host, and headliner at major hotels up and down Collins Ave from 185th on down to 1st street and back. That was the route. The beach run. Fifteen miles of ocean breeze, hot crowds, and showroom clubs with mics and stages. He was a regular at the Thunderbird Resort Motel, a favorite hangout of music industry professionals like Leonard Chess. They had free parking. Shore started out in local nightlife in 1957 in the Castanet Lounge at the Seville Hotel, billed as Chicago's Favorite Comedian. After that, he could be seen at the Bal Masque Supper Club at the Americana Hotel. Never a cover. Dinner show at 9. Supper show at midnight. The poster called him America's Newest Comedian, in a thumbnail of his silly face, profiled in a pressed shirt, dark jacket, and black tie. There he was in the Coach Room at the old Colonial

Inn Resort Motel up on 181st street in Sunny Isles Beach. Place had an orchestra led by Gene Carlton. Sammy could be found in the Flamenco Room of the Barcelona Hotel, over near where the Fontainebleau is today on the ocean from 43rd to 44th street. No cover. No minimum. Which goes to show that the two drink minimum is a social construct without a fundamental tradition in reality, and so is the cover charge. During the golden age of Miami comedy, no cover, no minimums was the norm. It was Sammy Shore on a show with a Cuban Nightingale backed by a full orchestra. Classy show. He could be found in the Eden Roc Hotel in their Pompeii Room in the hot and out-of-season middle of the summer. The, "Most beautiful supper club in the world," alongside belly dancing Egyptian Sisters, and the Academy Award winning star of Sayonara, Miyoshi Umeki. Never a cover charge, closed Mondays. And best of all, according to summer policy, full course deluxe dinner for $4.95. Mitzi Shore went to a lot of these shows, observing a variety of people and situations that added to her encyclopedic comedy brain as the owner of the Comedy Store on the Sunset Strip in LA, later on when Sammy moved to Vegas and she took over.

Who knows why they left Miami. It was a competitive market, the winter season entertainment capital of America. Even in April, Shore was up against Belle Barth at the Bel Aire, B.S. Pully at the Place Pigalle, the sexy stripper Evelyn West, "With her $50,000 Treasure Chest. Greatest of the G String Artists," at the original 5 O'Clock Club. There were dog races at the Biscayne Kennel Club, an amateur striptease contest at the Gaiety, lusty club owner Patsy Abbott on 23rd street, Twenty Arabian Beauties at the Club Morocco, Underwater Exotic Girls at the Casbah, Harry The Hipster at the Hi Room, the Voodoo Revue at the Jungle Club, a Havana Mardi Gras at The Lucerne, and more naked dancing striptease "burlesk" (sic. burlesque) girls than you could throw a million bucks at from the city to the beach. Funnily enough, toward the end of their time in Miami, Sammy Shore got into community theater before moving his young family to Los Angeles.

In 1970, he came back to town and opened for Elvis Presley at the Miami Beach Auditorium. He was cool with Presley's manager Col. Tom Parker, and of course Presley himself.

In 1973, Sammy opened for the 4 Tops at the Marco Polo and got slammed in a review by the Herald Entertainment Editor at the time Candice Russell, who said, "Lackluster comic Sammy Shore…unfunniest act I care to remember…material hackneyed…imitations trite…tired running joke…trying hard to whip up a roomful of laughter….one or two imaginative lines can't obscure the offensiveness of his leopard imitation…."

"Offensiveness of his leopard imitation," she said. What an idiot. Probably why nobody ever heard of her. Sammy Shore had hundreds of writeups in the Miami Herald and the Miami News working all the best rooms as a headliner. That does not happen by accident or by not being funny. Not to say that he never bombed a set, but repeat headline status can only be earned through making audiences laugh, have a good time, and tell people about it. Especially in Miami, which has always been and still is a word-of-mouth town even today.

By 1963 he was in at the Chez Paree in Chicago; the Copacabana and Latin Casino in New York; Thunderbird in Las Vegas; Eden Roc in Miami Beach; San Juan Hotel in Puerto Rico; and the entire Playboy Club chain. From at least 1963 on, his favorite jokes were printed with his photo and bio and syndicated nationally in a well read feature of the papers at the time. Guy was a proven commodity. Breezy Point Lodge, Brainer Minnesota, 1950. Zodiac in St Louis with Chamaco and his Latin Rhythm. At the Turin Inn in Sioux City, Iowa in 1951, "Young and funny comedian held over by popular request." At Pine Point Resort in Sheboygan, Wisconsin in 1952. At the Copa in Pittsburgh, the Esquire Red Room in Dayton, the Elbow Room in Windsor, Ontario, Canada in 1954. Harry and Alma's Supper Club in Detroit, Michigan in 1955. In 1956, he had his own tv show across Michigan. He was at the Celebrity Room in Philly in 1957. These are just highlights. It's over thousand search hits. And then he moved his fam to Miami, went all-county and tri-county with it, and kept touring.

So, pretty much, fuck the critics. Not that they're always wrong, just that they don't matter. If they're a good critic, their opinion is wrapped up in the truth of the historical details, so whether you agree or disagree, you can still learn from what they had to say. But they don't matter. The only critics that matter are the audience. If you can win the audience that's always louder than any critic. But comedy disappears in thin air, so all these articles and show announcements, listings, club ads, books, interviews, albums, tv shows, are the clues that helps us see the past so that we can be the future.

Sammy Shore showed up to Miami with a bang, commanding attention. According to Herb Kelly in the Amusements section of the

Miami News on April 17, 1958, "When comic Sammy Shore starts out, his jokes can be classed as earthy, which means they should be buried! Once he gets away from pleading for laughs and settles down to work he is capable. He's got a flash, particularly his "Saints" number. With all his faults, the audience loved him."

With all his faults, the audience loved him is the best that can be said of any comedian.

WALTER WINCHELL says:

"The Place Pigalle had over 400 patrons in one night following the rave here for its sensational stars, Sweet Richard and Princess Kitty from the Bahamas . . . Uninhibited Adam and Evil." —N.Y. MIRROR—DEC. 1

". . . Place Pigalle has one of the most exciting girly shows of all. It stars Sweet Richard and Princess Kitty (amazing limbo dancers from the Bahamas). An act packed with perpetual motion and very sinful!" —N.Y. MIRROR—NOV. 23

PAUL BRUUN: "Miami Beach's Number One Act is 'SWEET RICHARD and PRINCESS KITTY' " — M.B. SUN — NOV. 29

SWEET RICHARD
and
PRINCESS KITTY

King and Queen of the Limbo—

WILD and RAW FROM THE BAHAMAS

See THE FRENZIED FIRE DANCE IN ALL ITS PRIMITIVE COLOR AND PASSION!

FIRST SHOW 9 P.M.

NO COV. NO ADM.

30 EXOTIC DOLLS

CONT. 'TIL 5 A.M.

THE COMEDY KING OF BURLESQUE
TOMMY "MOE" RAFT WITH AL GOLDEN
"MISS PLAYGIRL OF 1960" — RANDY SCOTT
JAPAN'S NO. 1 FAN DANCER — SAYRONA
PLUS OUR *French Follies*

Place Pigalle

215 22nd St., M.B. Res. JE 8-0055

MEMBER: DINERS AM. EXPRESS AND HILTON

PRESENTS NIGHTLY:

GENE THE HAT AND HIS JAZZ QUARTET
SAM AMBROSE AND THE AFRO-BEATS
FLIP WILSON — MR. COOL HIMSELF

DANCING ALL NIGHT

22nd St. at Park Ave., M.B. JE 8-2294

3 DAYS ONLY FRI. SAT.-SUN.

Columbia Recording Star

ARETHA FRANKLIN

"Rock A Bye Your Baby With a Dixie Melody"

Coming Attraction NOV 9-10-11 LLOYD PRICE and his 15-piece BAND

MASTER OF CEREMONIES PHIL HARRIS

DANCING — FOOD

OPEN 'TIL 5:00 A.M.

★ CHICKIE HORNE Comedy

★ SAM EARLY His Hammond Organ and BAND

YOU MUST BE 21 AND PROVE IT

Johnny Lomelo's

KING O' HEARTS CLUB

6000 N.W. 7th AVE.
RES. PL 8-2339

LOMELO'S KING O'HEARTS

6000 N.W. 7th Ave.

Presents Miami's LARGEST

ROCK and ROLL JAM SESSION

5 BANDS CONTINUOUS ENTERTAINMENT

★ JOHNNY REX and his BOBSTERS ★

$1.00 GENERAL ADMISSION

FREE BEER ON DRAFT DURING SESSION

SUNDAY FROM 5 TO 9

NO MINORS ADMITTED

Johnny Lomelo's . . . It's new — "Couple Night" starting Monday — Prizes

KING O' HEARTS CLUB

THIS WEEK END 6000 N.W. 7th Avenue FEBRUARY 1 - 2 - 3

THE BIG SHOW SAM & DAVE Welcome HOME

PLUS . . . CHICKIE HORNE . . ORETHA REESE . . SAM EARLY . .

PHIL HARRIS . . HAZEL The Bimini Girl LEE EDDY New Singing Sensation

Monday night Admission FREE — Tables FREE – 3 pc. Men's Suit FREE

LAST FOUR DAYS

THURS - FRI - SAT - SUN

TO SEE AND HEAR

· CHICKIE HORNE

Special Bon Voyage Party Sunday Nite

CLUB MI

1900 N.W. 75th St.

Last Chance to Hear The
King of Liars

· FLIP WILSON

Held Over
Song Stylist

Little Clara Jay Dave Bondu, M. C.

Dance to the music of W. C Baker

Call PL 1-5951 for Reservation. Adm. 50c

Social clubs, organizations, fraternities—Club MI is available for your dance or banquet. Reasonable prices. All new Show Next Week

SEPT. 25-26-27

(FRI.-SAT.-SUN.)

COMEDY STAR DIRECT FROM A 6 WEEK RECORD-BREAKING ENGAGEMENT AT NEW YORK'S VILLAGE VANGUARD.

'FLIP' WILSON

CO-STARRING

Chickie Horne

FAMED AS "EFFIE THROCKBOTTOM"

All-Sepian Revue

2 GREAT BANDS 2

Frank DuBois' Chicken Scratchers

Freddie Scott's Scottsmen

SIR JOHN HOTEL

Knightbeat

276 N.W. 6th ST. MIAMI
PHONE: FR 3-3281

DON'T MISS EFFIE
AT THE

JIM JAM CLUB

FRIDAY - SATURDAY - SUNDAY

Chickie Horne's Revue

Featuring Bill Robinson and his Quails and Blues Songstress Etta Jones—Flip Wilson, Your Host

FLIP WILSON

One day in March of 1968, standup comic Flip Wilson was sitting first class in an airplane over Florida when it got hijacked. Two gunmen got up midair and forced the plane to Havana, Cuba. It was a trend at the time, with around twenty-five skyjackings in 1968 alone. Two guys with funny accents and .45 automatics were the culprits. Their mission was to deliver the screaming passenger who went hysterical that they were gonna kill him. Poor schlub sat down crying next to Flip. When the plane landed in Cuba, he chugged every half drank cup of beer, wine, and liquor on the way out and disappeared. Cuban military interrogated everyone else, fed them rice and beans, and sent them back to Miami where Flip Wilson stepped off looking sharp, if a little tired around the eyes, followed by a hippie with a bongo drum, according to the Miami Herald. It's funny, but two years later he had the biggest show on TV, and his career was really taking off. Twenty-five appearances on Johnny Carson, including as guest host. He got a one-hour network special, followed by his own show on NBC. First black American with his own network tv show. He struck gold. Exceeded all corporate expectations. Millions tuned in, and the next week millions more. A two year upward trending graph that hit a fifty-million live viewers a week spike before sliding in the ratings in the third season and getting canceled after four. Flip owned his own production company, and Little David Records label, and sold millions of albums (distributed by Atlantic), including George Carlin's seven dirty words bit on Class Clown. George Carlin was a staff writer on the Flip Wilson show, and Richard Pryor was too, giving them early opportunities and solid paychecks. They met when they all got high together backstage of a cheesy tv comedy special. Sponsored by Kraft. They were writers. At the time, Carlin was a square and Richie Pryor was considered a wimp, believe it or not. In 1983, Flip hosted Saturday Night Live, doing a famous sketch with a 22-year-old Eddie Murphy, who was around 12-years-old when he was watching Flip on tv. Wilson was a people's comic, and a comic's comic, regularly snorting coke, drinking, and smoking weed at his beachfront home in Malibu with Rodney Dangerfield and Redd Foxx. He had tons of broads, wives, and girlfriends, and a pile of kids, and he took care of all them. He drove a 1972 sky blue Rolls Royce Corniche convertible with plates that said KILLER, and he used to like to grab a few vials of pure, raw, uncut, 1970s, rich man's Los Angeles cocaine, a couple grams of hash, a box of pre rolled joints, and some cigarettes, and hit the road to Vegas or wherever else. Just drive, man, free.

And go look at real Americans and laugh. Go to the roadside no-name bars out in the desert, and drink double Cutty Sarks and smoke butt after butt of Pall Mall cigarettes. Look around. Take notes. It was a far ways from how he started out, but similar in more ways than one. In 1956, with a wad of cash, and a suitcase, he set off traveling by car, bus, train, on foot, and hitchhiking, to the spiritual home of his early days in comedy in Miami, Florida. The way I know this is that in 1956, the Miami Times newspaper advertised him as the "Comedy find of the year!" in a three column showbill for what looks like a rockin' party including Lord Flea and His Calypso Orchestra, and "Sensational interpretive dancing from Vicki Copez," at Club Basin Street, which was an old Mafia hotel. It was first called the Lord Calvert, named after a liquor distillery. I learned this from one of the owners of the club it became, the Sir John Hotel with its Knight Beat Club. The Sir John Knight Beat for short. Go to the corner of N.W. Sixth Street between second and third avenue in Miami, Florida today. It's a U.S. Post Office, and every time you open a P.O. Box, you can hear Sam and Dave singing "Soul Man." Like putting your ear to a seashell at the sea shore. I had a PO Box there for fourteen years until the price went up too high. Better than a jukebox. All the way to when the mob owned the place, before they sold it to a Miami Beach banker who had been a Nebraska homicide detective. Shout out Ben Danbaum. Back when it was called the Basin Street for that short time, after the Calvert, but before the Knight Beat, continuing that long tradition of club names that have no relation to the city they're in, Basin Street being a famous stem in New Orleans. Admission to see Flip was fifty cents, or seventy five cents on weekends. Hours were from twelve noon to five a.m. and liquor bottles were available at package-store prices with free tables for everybody. Now that's a great deal on drinks and entertainment.

It was a different city at the time. Rhumba was in the air, but there wasn't a Latin majority yet. That process would begin with the first wave of Cuban expats fleeing the Cuban Revolution in 1959. This was the time before the U.S. highway came and ran through the U.S. population like a crosscut saw. Before civil rights and integration opened up the formerly all-white entertainment venues to all Americans for the green faces in their wallets and purses. It was a small town with a constant flow of new arrivals and excitement. The Magic City on the swingin' head of Florida where there was money flowing on both sides of the bridge, and it went back into the community. Flip moved to Miami in 1956 and made fast friends in Overtown, just north of downtown, full of 40,000 people on the west side of the train tracks. The nightlife and entertainment scene documented through national features and regular reporting in Jet, Ebony, and other long form publications with photography, like LIFE Magazine's iconic photos by Flip Schulke of 19 year old Muhammad Ali throwing punches under water in the Sir John Hotel pool. The NAACP Crisis Magazine published a major article in the 1920s detailing life, economics, pioneers, and culture in black Miami. When Flip arrived, Miami was a known free speech capital. For example, Reverend Theodore Gibson did six months in jail for going up against the FBI when he refused to show them the registration rolls of NAACP membership, for which he was ultimately found constitutionally protected by the first amendment. First vilified, then heroized. He has a park named after him today. One of Flip's biggest characters was Reverend Leroy, so he was always watching clergy to pick up on their mannerisms, speech patterns, cadences, body language. The city was known for sunshine, the ocean, and proximity to the Caribbean. For economic prosperity in a state rife with racial violence. For its concentration of black wealth and power. D.A. Dorsey, millionaire. For pioneering families, Knights, Pinders, Williams, Glovers, Sands, Sawyers, Jones, Ingrahams, Rolles, Sweetings, Alburys,

Adderleys, Culmers, Bullards, Munnings, Carrols, Armbristers, Colebrooks, Ranges, Stirrups, and many more bringing a raw wilderness into urban modernity, and through arduous eras of slums and slum clearance. Plumbing. Garbage collection. Schools. Police. Concrete streets. For its gospel, its port, its civic organizations, its football games, its entrepreneurs, its architecture, and its opportunity. Bronzetown U.S.A., a Sepia capital just like Central Ave in L.A., South Side Chicago, Black Indianapolis, Harlem, Oklahoma City, Philly, Detroit, Atlanta, Baltimore, East St. Louis, New Orleans, Houston. Many more. Little towns nobody ever heard of. In 1957, Flip helped Miami Times newspaper columnist Dave "Mr. Swing" Bondu while he was on vacation. He wrote neighborhood-news and human interest pieces for the Miami Times, including one about pioneering Overtown club promoter Frank LeGree (who was the first black home-owner in Orchard Villa, Liberty City, and famously busted a group of white supremist crossburners on his front lawn ((never fuck with a black motherfucker's front lawn)) by jumping out on them from behind a bush with the cops). Flip wrote a column on local radio DJ Milton "Butterball" Smith, who used to make love to and respectfully, fuck the shit outta Aretha Franklin when she recorded and performed in Miami. Used to make love to her and cook her fried chicken and she would scream his name all through the halls if he was late and wail on that piano; Then he would go and play her record on the radio over and over for the people all night long. Flip also reported on a trip he took to Pompano, FL with baseball king Satchel Paige as he opened a new community center up there in Broward County. He wrote about a local reverend and his family and a talented piano player named Nathaniel "Nat" Jones, and he made self deprecating jokes about his own bad grammar and spelling.

His people skills kept him going through tough times. A fortunate turn of events was when a Miami Beach businessman named Herbie Shul saw him perform and offered to invest $50 a week in Flip's career, no tax, no viggorish. It sounded like a setup, but Shul was legit. He saw an investment angle, but Flip paid him back all his bread before he was even a millionaire. When they met, Flip was broke and hungry, sleeping on the hoods of random Cadillacs (how big cars used to be) along NW 2nd Ave in Overtown when he didn't have the $20 a week to stay at the Sir John Hotel or a rooming house. So he accepted Shul's investment, as well as a line he had on a gig at the Cat N' Fiddle club a wave's hop away in Nassau, Bahamas.

It was 1957, Flip was on a two-week run of shows at the hottest club in Nassau when he met a pretty dancer named Peaches, and a few weeks later, he married her, earning a newspaper shoutout from Dave Bondu in the Miami Times on March 16, 1957, with Flip quoted as saying, "Good wine, good conch, and no tv, man, you're bound to get hooked." His wife's real name was Patricia Dean. Her brother was a famous entertainer called Richard Dean who had a lucrative act with his wife: Sweet Richard and Princess Kitty, that worked mostly out of the Place Pigalle on Miami Beach, a Borsht Belt cum Florida hotbed of sexed up humor, exotic dancing girls, and tropical entertainments open till 5a.m. nightly. Sweet Richard was featured in comic-book-like advertisements where he held a knife in his teeth like a pirate and Princess Kitty was over him in a bikini with a long string of shells and a smile. They were, "King and Queen of the Limbo. Wild and raw from the Bahamas in all its primitive color and passion," until one day after a show, Sweet Richard downed a bottle of rum, choked on a piece of steak, and met his untimely demise in a suite on South Beach. Showbiz is dangerous. RIP.

In 1959, Flip booked a month of gigs at the Rocking MB at 22nd and Park on Miami Beach, at a white club that promoted black entertainment, Pete Clark and The Blues, Gene The Hat, Sam Ambrose and The Afro-Beats. George Kirby worked there too. Bold print in the Miami Herald said, "Flip Wilson - Mr. Cool Himself" in an advertisement that ran every day for twenty five days straight. Not cheap, even back then. The club was in the same few blocks as Belle Barth's Pub, and Murray Franklin's. More on them later. The Rocking MB was operated by Bucky Gray. In 1952, State Beverage Agents grabbed five minors when they left the club and arrested them, even though they were allowed to be there. Maybe Detective Art Leonard and C.W. Huddleston didn't like seeing jazz, bebop, and jam sessions with no cover and no minimum in Vanderbilt Square at 2027 Collins Ave. In 1955, Bucky Gray was one of the six officers of the corporation (dissolved in 1962) operating the Rocking MB Bar. They were named in an indictment for the charge of selling liquor to minors. The business pulled through. Trumpet king Dizzy Gillespie and his quintet held down a two week residency there in 1959, followed by Cozy Cole and Earl Bostic. Not too much later it closed.

Flip was in Miami at the right time, with a name and a voice in the heart of the city, and a buzz on the beach, he could tour the east coast up to Boston, like he did with soul singer Betty Wright's brother's band, the Calypso themed Downbeats, at Jay's Lounge on Boylston Street for a three month stand. Or he could hop over to the Caribbean.

The Bahamas are closer to Miami than Miami is to New York City, so there was a lot of back and forth in the Caribbean circuit that included Cuba, and Puerto Rico. There was a lot of mob money involved, from all the different mobs operating. The Italians, the Jews, the Black Mafia up in Harlem, and their Liberty City counterparts who were often from Mississippi, The Carolinas, and Georgia. Then there were the Cubans, the Bahamians, the Chicago guys, the Philly guys, the Detroit guys, the Jamaicans, all these different factions working all their different cash businesses in entertainment in Miami at the same time. There was pharmaceutical grade cocaine and flocks of quacks prescribing a sordid bevy of methamphetamines, barbiturates and their compounds and derivatives for pill popping or injecting. There was grass coming in from Jamaica, and Chinese heroin, or black tar Mexican coming from Frisco or LA or Texas, or directly to the Port of Miami or Tampa Bay in large quantities from the Golden Triangle via the Cuban Mafia. Lots of good, strong liquor, Havana Club, Bacardi from the island. As much beer as anyone could care to drink. Champagne by the pallet. Caviar by the caseload. Lobster mobsters and shrimp barons.

Drop-shippers, bootleggers, and offloaders. Comedy in a party town. There were dice games in every alley, jokers in every deck, spades on every corner, and gold on every street, with sidewalks glowing in the neon wash of opportunity. Aged Cohiba Cigars from Havana filled the smokey casinos and all night pool halls up and down the coast. Illegal lotto houses were running numbers, especially out of Overtown and Hialeah, where Cubans coined the term and everybody fell in and started calling it Bolita. Everybody loved Bolita. Back when winning digits were called out through coded messages on live radio and through mysterious classified announcements built from randomized horse track data and subliminal messages in the newspapers, hand collected and delivered with proof slips that either hit for payday or blew off in the wind like trash.

By the time Flip arrived in 56', a politician named Kefauver, who was head of the U.S. Senate committee investigating organized crime, had managed to shut down the beachfront casinos in a failed attempt to run the mob out of town, so the game changed but it stayed the same.

You could still bet the ponies and the dogs at the Kennel Club, or Hialeah, or Tropical Park, or Gulfstream, or any number of other fine courses and tracks in Dade, Broward, and Palm Beach Counties. You might even see future TV interviewer Larry King staking everything on a trifecta. One second he was a drunk loser. The next second he was fifty racks up, in 1950s money. The casinos were gone but the party wasn't over. All the newspapers were full of nightlife ads like the many that appeared for the King O' Hearts, which was at one time an all white rock'n'roll and dirty-dancing club from when Liberty City was a mostly white neighborhood, to the dancehall it became when it turned to a wide-open soul-powered rhythm-rockin', hard knockin', wap-laugha-wooha-bop-bam-boom of a party spot. The club pivoted with the changing demographics in the area. Owner John Lomelo declared to the Herald that he was going black. Cops and officials tried to dissuade him, constantly violating him with inspections, charges, fines, and sweeps by Beverage Agents when he ignored their instructions to keep it white and he'd be alright. The Florida State Beverage Department was created by the Beverage Act of 1935, which provided the authority to tax and regulate the liquor industry. High school teens and young adults were constantly trying to get in the club and sometimes succeeding, resulting in underage violations in addition to at least one charge of diluting liquor. In 1960, "Burglars stole $400 in whiskey, $500 in change from a jukebox, and $100 in change from a cigarette machine." Bar business wasn't easy. But over the years, the King O'Hearts brought in pioneer DJ Butterball Smith, Clyde McPhatter from The Drifters, Lloyd Price who did "Personality," Little Esther with her "Double Crossing Blues," Bill Robinson and The Quails with "Lay Your Head On My Shoulder," Al Hibbler with his "Unchained Melody," The Drifters sang "Under The Boardwalk," Little Willie John hit that "Fever," Sam Early with some of the best local Hammond organ, Oretha Reese was a local vocalist, W.C. Baker had the neighborhood blues, Phil Harris was a popular M.C., Aretha Franklin who got her "Respect," Solomon Burke sang "Cry To Me," Hazel The Bimini Girl was a fine exotic dancer, Sam and Dave from the Hall of Fame ready for "Soul Man," and "Hold On." It was a hot club.

Ahmet Ertegun and Jerry Wexler from Atlantic Records heard about it, and were in there at different times checking for talent. That's how they came to sign Sam and Dave. Sammy Moore and Dave Prater played all over Miami, Cuba, and The Bahamas, doing covers and performing at what were essentially gangster parties with the shows booked by their manager, who was John Lomelo, either promoted by family dollars or for entertainment at their jams. The way that Sam

& Dave fit on the whole comedy scene is that they were there on a lot of the shows back then that had mixed bills of comedy and music, so as they got started and grew with that whole generation of entertainers, Sam Moore and Dave Prater got to be friends and hang out with Flip Wilson, and Richard Pryor, and George Kirby, and Redd Foxx, Nipsey Russell, even, and Bill Cosby, Stu Gilliam, and Scoee Mitchell; and Wildman Steve, who MC'd their big show at Dinner Key Auditorium. Talented women were very prominent in Miami with Aretha, Nina, Billie, Ella, Marion Williams, Ruth Brown, Dinah Washington, Tina Turner, Big Maybelle, Eartha Kitt, Patti LaBelle, Dionne Warwick, Betty Wright, Helene Smith, Clara Ward, Vanilla Williams, Elois Forman. There were too many civic organizations to count. Alberta Sawyer owned the Mary Elizabeth Hotel, Elizabeth Virrick made the govt clean the streets, Lady Sax in Opa Locka didn't own the nightclub Harlem Gardens, but she ran the whole show. Lotta women strongly connected various ways.

Even some who looked like them.

Chickie Horne used to be in the King O' Hearts as Effie Throckbottom, an MC, comedian, musical entertainer, and party host whose act went everywhere from Jamaica to

England to New York City, but especially Miami, Florida, as a headline entertainer with a big personality and chest to match. Little Richard with tits and an attitude. There's hardly a week during the golden era of soul, funk, and r&b that Chickie's name and picture weren't on some show poster in the Miami Times, that's how popular Chickie Horne was. Every week. Chickie was a Character. With a capital C. And a hit with the everyday people most of all. It wasn't fun and games in the streets of Overtown. Guys like "Flossie," a female impersonator who the Miami Times said was, "Found in a pool of blood in his apartment at 263 NW 6th St, shot to death. Death was caused by gun shot wounds in the head and chest. Police found a long list of telephone numbers." Horne worked clubs all over the city, matter of fact, that very same day that Flossie was on the front page for getting murdered, Chickie Horne was on page 3 in furs and a party dress, in a quarter page ad for a show at Club MI at 1900 NW 75th street in the hood of Liberty City. On that very same bill, "Last chance to hear the King of Liars - Flip Wilson." Chickie Horne stayed in the city or performed on the beach if the money was right, or if it was a good cause. Miami was known for mixed parties. The only city in America where the Native Americans never signed a treaty with the U.S. Government. Way before “integration,” all audiences were generally welcome in certain spaces that dared to promote it, as evidenced by advertising and reporting in the Miami Times, the Miami Herald, and the Miami News, as well as a former Sir John Knight Beat club owner Sonia “Sonny” Rabin telling me directly that the Gray Line Tour Bus used to pick up full loads of tourists from hotels on Ocean Drive and drop them off at the Knight Beat to party. Dave Bondu, a writer for the Miami Times who was also a show promoter and radio deejay alongside his wife Mayme, documented much of it in hundreds of newspaper columns he wrote, in photos he took, and show announcements with his name. Newspaper ads had directions on how to get to the hood, such as, "Hampton House. From Miami Beach, take 36th St to 27th Ave. American Express Accepted." Reason being is, City of Miami Beach is an island off the City of Miami; they are separated by several bridges over the troubled waters of Biscayne Bay. But the only color that matters in South Florida is money. Paper dollars, credit cards, travelers checks, gold. Don’t be green. Spend it. Miami Herald. December 1955. “Club Calvert. Miami’s Most Exciting Niteclub. White and Colored Welcome! All audiences, all races Welcome.” 1956, "America's Newest Comic Sensation, Slappy White, 4 shows nightly, last show 3a.m. White & Colored Guests Welcome!"

1958, at the Jim Jam, "All are welcome." This era of Miami was when dynamite attacks by the KKK and other white supremacists still occurred with violent frequency. America wanted blood. Especially in Florida, where the KKK grand dragon lived in Tallahassee, and Miami led the nation for racial bombings. Miami Herald 1957: "Will Dynamite Set Off Racial War In Miami?" Nitroglycerine attacks around Brownsville, Liberty City, and NE Miami made local and national news. The targets were black housing and black churches and jew temples. A ghost named Kasper came to town and tried to burn it to the ground. With kerosene he lit up crosses, but news is bad for crime bosses. It's all for profit, no losses. So he had to go, for being dead obvious. By 1963, even Lee Winfrey from the Miami Herald had to admit, "The Knight Beat is Miami's first integrated nightclub. Other local nightspots catering to both whites and Negroes are the Hampton House, 4200 NW 27th Ave., and the King O' Hearts Club, 6000 NW Seventh Ave."

When Flip showed up, the King O' Hearts had been through a lot. It had been a burlesk joint, then a rockabilly club, then the former owner Ernie Shufflebarger's wife got killed by a drunk driver early one morning when she was walking across the street outside the club. Then the Lomelo family came to town from

New Jersey and bought the place. John Lomelo got the keys from his father, and opened the doors to all talent, and the talent exploded. Just between Sam Moore and Dave Prater and Flip Wilson, local acts that cut their teeth at the King O' Hearts dominated mainstream radio and television, insuring continuous relevance in perpetuity as the historic wheel re-introduces their cultural contributions to new audiences. But this book here is all about where those original contributions came from, even finding out things a lot of experts don't know. John Lomelo was a tough guy who was arrested for multiple capers and heists, found guilty of armed robbery at the Coral Bar and Grill for holding the operator at gunpoint and taking sixty bucks after convincing the waitress to get him in there. Five year prison sentence, released on bond for six months, suspended sentence. Never did a day in jail. Lomelo's mother was Czech. His father was Italian. "Retired USPS." People said he was connected. In another arrest, Lomelo Jr.'s car was searched by the robbery squad and twenty thousand dollars in stolen gold from a jewelry store heist was found. Charges dismissed. Three years later, accessory after the fact for armed robbery. Charges dropped. His father made things happen. Lomelo got off with a dirty rap sheet, a loaded reputation, and a few potentially business-damaging news articles.

Maybe they helped. Who knows. Lomelo liked to brag that the retaliation for having such a hot club led to his getting arrested eighteen times, but no convictions. Worst of all though was the time his pistol fell out of his waistband and shot him through his own chest while he was talking to some cops through their car window outside his club. He barely made it to Jackson Memorial Hospital on time and the bullet came a hair's breadth from exploding his aorta. Turns out John Lomelo really was the king of hearts. In 1963, he sold the KOH and it became the Continental Club. Lomelo and his wife went north-west of Dade County, and in short order, he became the first Mayor of Sunrise, FL, up the line in Broward County. One of his accomplishments was building the Sunrise Musical Theater (more on that later) and financing it through aggressive expansion, before his eventual indictment on corruption charges. True Florida pioneer, and a lot of people still love and miss him. Anyway, Lomelo had a solid open-door policy for talent, and Chickie Horne used to work his club with anyone and everyone who came through there, including Flip Wilson. Black people get a bad rap for being homophobic, but it's not that true. Chickie Horne could be seen at clubs such as the Sir John Knight Beat, the Jim Jam Club, the Mi Club, the King O' Hearts, the Harlem Square, the Fiesta Room, the Hampton House, the Peppermint Lounge, the Island Club, the Continental, the Miami Beach Auditorium, the Rancher, and many more. With Sam & Dave and Aretha Franklin. With NFL star Roosevelt Grier. With Chuck Jackson and Flip Wilson. Hundreds if not thousands of documented shows over more than a decade with the now legendary R&B stars who partied and performed in Miami since it was founded.

This is significant because Flip Wilson't most famous character was not Rev. Leroy from the Church of What's Happening Now, but rather Geraldine, a sassy southern belle who wore designer clothes, had a way with words, and an unseen boyfriend named Killer, that was revealed to be OJ Simpson in the Flip show's final episode.

Wilson variously credited screen actress Butterfly McQueen, and a neighborhood West-Indian girl in Jersey City, amongst other influences for his Geraldine character's voice, which had appeared on his standup comedy records and live act for years, since he first started actually. But it was his tv special that showed her to people for the first time and the way I found out is that people who were there in Overtown when it was happening told me he got that from Chickie Horne. Sam Moore from Sam and Dave told me that. Steve

Alaimo who hosted a national tv show called Where The Action Is said so too. Joyce Moore triple confirmed it. And the streets of Miami verified it. All I know is, they definitely worked together in the early days, and Chickie Horne was a headliner when Flip Wilson was an open mic guy. However, by 1964, the tables had turned. A newspaper ad from September of that year says, "Flip Wilson, comedy star from a six week record-breaking engagement at New York's Village Vanguard, co-starring Chickie Horne, famed as Effie Throckbottom. All Sepian Revue. 2 Great Bands. Sir John Hotel Knight Beat. 276 NW 6th St."

The Geraldine character had plenty of haters. People saw it as a white corporate conspiracy to demasculate the black man. They're still talking about it today. But the joke's on the haters, because it came from their own tradition. Geraldine won crowds over in nightclubs across America, from Stockton, California to Miami Beach, Overtown, Liberty City, Chicago, Detroit, NYC. When audiences laugh it means it's funny. Critics don't mean shit.

Comic in a dress is one of the oldest gags ever. It's a gimmick old as fart jokes. Anything for a laugh. That's comedy. The only thing that bothered Flip about it was everyone asking him to do her all the time everywhere he went. That's what got on his nerves.

When he started out, it was all jokes all the time. On the talent show circuit with two guys named Samuel Moore and Dave Prater, Sam & Dave, the basis for the Blues Brothers characters from that famous movie and its soundtrack. Number one soul duo all time. Stax Records. Isaac Hayes. David Porter. Atlantic Records. Backed by Booker T & The MGs. "Hold On, I'm Comin'," "Soul Man!" "When Something's Wrong With My Baby," the list goes on and on and on. Their explosive live show made raw-emotion popular. Soul was love and pain, with melody, rhythm, harmony, and funk. For example, December, 1960, after a remodeling and renovation, "Lomelo's King O' Hearts Club. The newest and most beautiful in Miami. Welcome FAMU and Langston fans. Special Classic Floor Show. Sammy Moore and Dave Prater, E. Lois Foreman, Phil "Untouchable" Harris. Flip Wilson, Master of Comedy. Open house. Saturday Matinee. Music by Fish Ray, The Sand Man, and His Calypsonians." That's a lot of history right there. The Orange Blossom Classic football game brought a week of entertainment to Miami. Like a Super Bowl in town every year. Sammy Moore, that's Miami's own, Overtown's own, church, and school, and home's own, got shot in the leg in

1954 bangin' someone else's old lady's own. 1455 NW 3rd Avenue's own. Sam Moore. Voice as big as Hercules was strong. Soul as bright as the burning sun. Pain as raw as the ocean salt on heartache. Resplendent in the Glory of the good he also does. Sam Moore. "When Something Is Wrong With My Baby," bring a tear to your eye. He needs his own chapter. His own book. He had it all, man, deals, and broads, and dollars, and drugs, and bills, that came time to pay up all too soon, but never soon enough to beat back the devil's portents, the one inside his mind, the one we've got trying to get all of us. He had the chance to lead the Soul Stirrers gospel group, but he chose the path of fame and stardom, popular music, a path besot with inequity, through whose obstacles he someday found redemption. He's here right now, watching you reading this very book, still very much alive, and heart beating strong to the beat of the drum of truth, beauty, love, soul, and comedy. That's who Flip Wilson started in Miami with.

1961. Flip Wilson is on the bill for a big show at The Hampton House, one of the most historic music venues in all Miami, even though it's in Brownsville, which is unincorporated. A land without title to the city it helped create. At one time, it was a black farming and hunting area. It became a white section that became a black upper-class neighborhood that the government built housing projects into, purposely driving down the residebtial property values, consisting of well built classic Florida architecture in single-family homes, many of which were built in the 40s and 50s and are still standing strong today. The Hampton House opened in July of 1954 as the Booker Terrace Motel, advertised as the 'first black luxury motel' in the United States. Five acre property with all rooms fully air conditioned. Built for $1,000,000 by a Jewish investor group and then bought out two years later by Harry and Florence Markowitz, a remarkable Jewish couple with a pioneering idea. They renamed it the Hampton House Motel and Villas, and it was a Green Book Motel, meaning it was included in a printed list of nationally safe-to-be-black establishments in the country. The Markowitz's were there, and worked every job in the place. Radio DJ China Valles, who Duke Ellington called The Mahj (short for Maharaja (("Great King" in Sanskrit)), often broadcast live from the jazz lounge) and all the hep cats and cool chicks in-the-know were welcome. The Hampton House had 99 rooms, 28 with kitchens, a meeting hall for 200, swimming pool, cocktail lounge, and restaurant. That's after Harry Markowitz completed a $175,000 remodeling job on the place in 1961, telling the Miami Herald that he would advertise to attract black conventions. The Hampton House did honest business on cash and credit, which may be taken for granted now, but life was different at the time. Traveling professionals, vacationing tourists, touring musicians, and national political figures all stayed there. It was the time of dynamite fire-bombings, and cross-burnings by the KKK and others in and around that very neighborhood of Brownsville, at a time when plenty of white businesses still said, "No Dogs, No Jews, No Niggers Allowed" from downtown to the beach. During segregation, the Hamp held full integrated parties with everybody having a blast. The good kind. Amid terrible local police corruption and with the FBI closely following the activities of the Nation Of Islam, they welcomed Malcolm X. The Hampton House is where Muhammad Ali met Cap'n Sam and rose from the ashes of Cassius Clay like a pugilistic phoenix. It's where MLK practiced I Have A Dream looking onto Unity Boulevard through a concrete block screen, while pacing next to the pool, and people say he even had some wild times there as well cavorting with the ladies. MLK was friends with Butterball, and Butterball liked to have fun. There were 24 hour parties four days a week, with a 6a.m. jazz show packed with everyone in suits and gowns. Billie Holiday could be found scoring horse and nodding out on the all white bear-skin rug at the ultra luxe Georgette's Tea Room up the street, where she kept a permanent suite. Brownsville was prosperous. It's where the doctors, judges, and lawyers lived in well built old Florida houses with jalousie windows, porticos, and filigree, Florida Room screen enclosed porches, lion statues, bright paint, and forget the white pickets, think of steel spike fences in gold, black, or green. The Mafia was around, and they were always trying to get in on the action. So shout out to the Markowitzes. The Hampton House is now a National Historic Landmark Museum thanks to activist, filmmaker, and public educator Enid C. Pinkney and the Historic Hampton House Community Trust. Mrs. Pinkney herself stood in front of a wrecking ball that wanted to demolish the place after it fell to disrepair when it went out of business. Today it's a living museum and you can go take the tour.

In the 50s and 60's, The Hampton House regularly advertised in the Miami Times newspaper, paying into the black economy on a weekly basis, and the Miami Herald as well, contributing to the Knight family's wealth for that matter.

So quit saying Jews are never did anything for anybody! (I'm a Jew) an American Jew, not an Israeli)).

In 1961, Flip Wilson was the comedian MC at a party called La Petite Affaire at a show including a Haitian Fire Goddess, a limbo act, and a calypso combo, at the bar where Malcolm X, Nina Simone, Billy X, Big Maybelle, and MLK all hung out. There was Flip's face, smirking from the center of a full page ad in the newspaper.

1961, Wilson worked with Screaming Jay Hawkins ("I Put A Spell On You"), at the Mr. James Club on 36th street and NW 2nd Ave. Little Haiti border to Wynwood today. I lived in both those areas for years. Screaming Jay used to come out on stage in a coffin, people say he had fifty kids, and used to have a woman or two before every show. The two also performed together in the heart of Overtown at the Fiesta Room in the Mary Elizabeth Hotel for a three night stand with free admission!

It was all part of his fifteen year plan to get rich and famous as a comic. Pain and hunger. Putting in work, he planned to make it, quit, or die trying. Stage time and audience approval. Broad audiences for the sophisticated showcase artist. Flip played all different clubs. He wasn't strictly on the chitlin circuit. He played the black clubs anywhere he could, the black theatres of the major cities, whatever white or international rooms he could get into along the way, which were some big ones, and every television camera pointed at him, which got him even more.

In 1965, Johnny Carson asked Redd Foxx who the best young comic was, and Redd said, "Flip Wilson!" It was the beginning of a long and beautiful friendship. The first time he was on the show he got an uproarious reaction from the ugly baby story. "And I'll get a banana for your monkey too!" Big appearance. He became an American favorite on America's network. In 1968, Flip got a one hour special on NBC and dropped a standup album on Atlantic Records. In 1970, he got his own show and started his own record label.

The Miami News
July 16, 1970
Herb Kelly

From Rags To Riches

"It seems such a short time ago when Flip Wilson was scrounging a living playing the Knight Beat room in the Sir John Hotel for very short money. He worked the dives in

Miami and in Broward County for eating money, sharpening his experience as a comedian, correcting his mistakes and waiting for the big break. One time he was so flat broke he had to get his night's sleep in a nickel pay toilet. Times have changed and for the better. Flip has just put in a bid for a $300,000 mansion in Beverly Hills."

The first two years on air, Flip, was one of the biggest shows on tv, hitting 50 million live viewers weekly. America went for Geraldine so much it almost drove Flip crazy. They never did stop asking him for her. They're still at him today, standing at his grave site, talking about, "Do Geraldine!"

It got to be a burden on his psyche. See, Flip was a thinker. He was into the philosophy of Khalil Gibrani, who wrote a best-selling book called The Prophet. He was always reading in the Air Force, had a trunk full of books and liked to barter them out. And how he got his name was from a joke, a play on words from a famous line in Shakespeare's play Julius Caesar, which he read in his bunk and kept going back to. You can hear the bit that it developed into, the 'berry joke,' on different recordings, but it's a flip. The Shakespeare line is "I come to bury Caesar, not to praise him!" and Wilson came up with an over-long and complicated setup just as a way to say, "I come to seize her berry, not to praise it." Always testing and refining. Iterating and reiterating until he got the better rating. Eruption of laughter. Wilson flipped his lid. He flipped the script. They called him Flip. And it sticked.

He kept a book he was writing about his theories of comedy, and he found that the berry joke worked because a bad joke with a big buildup to set up a clever groaner made the audience like him more somehow. Charisma through self immolation.

In a dark comedic turn, Flip predicted his own death on a comedy record. It comes at the end of the recording, and it's a riff on cancer.

Clerow "Flip" Wilson grew up in rough circumstances, abandoned by his mother at seven years old, one of (slightly exaggerating) 25 kids supported by a single father working with a hammer, a shovel, a paintbrush, and a saw, standing on street corners, hustling work as a maintenance man. It was rough. All the youngsters got sent to group homes or foster homes of varying severity. The older kids mostly dispersed to the workforce. Flip ran off from so many foster homes and reform schools, that he carried whipping scars from when he was beat with cords as punishment so bad it hit him in his soul for the rest of his life. Check the closeups from his tv show, got some of that pain still in his eyes. Part of what made people like him. Forced to eat the nasty mash and scraps from other kids' dinner plates and live in their shadows, attics, and storage rooms while they drank his welfare milk, as he fought to survive in a sick and crazy world where women kept using him for money, and he was the only standup guy he knew. Flip lied about his age and joined the U.S. Air Force at age sixteen and finally got to eat three healthy meals a day for the first time in his life. Military discipline was a welcome respite from a life of chaos. He found himself late one night laying on his back on a baseball diamond at a military base in the South Pacific nation of Guam, high on heroin, pondering the mysteries of the universe. Military life. He sold a little dope, became an expert typist, and wrote a successful one-man-show on the Sex Habits of South Pacific Giant Coconut Crabs. Clean with an edge. It's how he learned to write for a general audience, clock the laughs, and tour. The Air Force let him do his crab-talk at various events to boost company morale. In four years, his contract was up, and he found work as a hotel bellhop in San Francisco, and then playing a silly drunk on stage between music acts as a comedy schtick in the hotel's nightclub. From there, he took his show on the road, developing a blockbuster act at Club 4 in Stockton, California as Reverend "Flip"

Wilson, according to a solid year and a half of newspaper advertisements with his name connected to multiple acts in that town, and a shoutout to some gigs he worked for the million-selling indie R&B jump-jazz composer Louis Jordan, leader of the Tympany Five.

But it was Miami that made him. Showed him a a taste of the good life and a stomping grounds full of funny characters and hilarious situations, easy access to smoke and coke, all the best talent in the world blowing into town and then leaving on a regular basis, steady gigs, amazing broads, clubs on top of clubs next to bars on top of bars, and the whole eastern seaboard available for moneymaking. A slice of paradise. Eventually, his career hit and he moved to LA to do the show. He had money. Owned houses. The nice one in Miami with the lake in the back yard where his ex-wife, a Miami girl named Blondell Pittman raised their four kids before he got custody in their divorce settlement. His NBC show, which was simply called Flip, lasted four years with ninety-four one-hour episodes produced by his own company; and he retained IP rights through negotiations and it made him a millionaire in his lifetime with a valuable catalog in the great hereafter, and a $20 million dollar estate when he passed away in 1998, a rare feat for an independent player in cut-throat Hollywood. The year before he died, he executed a multi million dollar deal for broadcast licensing of the Flip show to the TV Land network. Not bad for a Jersey City orphan. He was an investor with his original manager Monte Kay and made beaucoup money (which means, "a lot" in French), off Texas cattle ranching. Monte Kay was a funny cat, original founder of the Birdland jazz club in New York City before old school gangster Morris Levy from Roulette Records pushed him out of the place and took it over. Monte was a Jewish kid who dyed his skin with iodine to look black. He married a real nice looking, light complexion young actress named Diahann Carol, and people kept on trying to figure out what their deal was. They got divorced. Monte treated Flip good, but in the end, the cocaine-paranoia, the psychosis, took hold of Flip and he cut Monte out of his life. When they first, first met at the Apollo in Harlem, Monte said he would manage him and that he wouldn't take a dime until Flip was making seven hundred fifty a week (managers usually get 10% or 15-20% automatically), and he stayed true to his word and they made a lot of money together. When Flip got a speeding ticket on Route 66 while LIFE Magazine did a cover story on him, he laughed. Flip bought a hot air balloon, and went hot air ballooning over the Panama Canal, motorcycle riding in Hawaii, flying ultralight aircrafts over the desert, and piloting helicopters. All made possible by comedy. Television. And owning his intellectual property. The Flip show's format was variety: Standup comedy, monologues, skits, special guests, and musical numbers from top charting entertainers and star athletes. He put on for the soul and funk and standup community, paying every artist $7,500 to be on his show for a few minutes work; helping his fellow comics when they needed work, and going hard ninety hours a week to make it all happen. Flip helped get Redd Foxx in with NBC, which led to Sanford and Son. Everyone from James Brown to Aretha Franklin, Joe Namath, Moms Mabley, Ray Charles, Gina Lollobrigida, Muhammad Ali, Lola Falana, Slappy White, Jerry Stiller, Paul McCartney, Pointer Sisters, Gladys Knight, The Pips, Slappy White, B.B. King, Sugar Ray Robinson, Stevie Wonder, Joan Rivers, Lily Tomlin, Don Rickles, Ray Charles, The Supremes, The Temptations, The Fifth Dimension, James Brown, just to name a few and even the Muppets joined the fun. Flip had two of his writers, George Carlin and Richard Pryor on stage too. Check the laughs in Harry Belafonte, "Lime In The Coconut," a double reverse on the Harry Nilsson classic. Redd Foxx "Belligerent Drunk." Bobbie Darrin played the Devil in a hilarious edition of the Church Of What's Happening Now, an extended riff on religious profiteering; Flip's own comedic and often imitated parallel to the famous Lenny Bruce bit Religions Inc. The Reverend Leroy character first appears in print when Flip was in Stockton, where he was advertised as Rev. Flip Wilson in 1954 in the Stockton Daily Evening Record. He kept developing the voice over fifteen years of club and theater dates, and The Church Of What's Happening Now exploded in popularity as the caricature writ large over several nationwide seasons of call and response, loud, in charge sloganeering, and subversive social satire, before plateauing and then falling off. It was an exciting and creative time, but it did not come easy. From 1956 to 1970, Flip Wilson had a life and home in Miami, but lived out of a suitcase, performing in Harlem at the Apollo Theater; in DC at the Howard Theatre; in Chicago at the Regal Theater; in Troy, New York at the Skyview Lodge; in Philly at the Uptown; in Baltimore at the Stanton; in San Francisco at the Sugar Hill or the Hungry I; in Boston at Lennie's; in Cincinnati at the Living Room; in NYC at the Vanguard, or the Monday Night Jazz Jam at Morris Levy's Birdland, opposite Charles Mingus with his 13 piece orchestra; with Dizzy Gillespie and Muddy Waters at the Mosque Theatre in New Jersey; in Detroit at the Riviera; or in any of Hugh Hefner's Playboy Clubs across the country. Over Virginia at the Market Inn, Flip was advertised in the Richmond News Leader in 1962 as "The Greatest Comic On Earth." But whenever he took that old suitcase home, that home was in Miami, Florida, where he had four kids who he loved and cared for with a woman he spent seventeen years (of an open relationship) with. Geraldine helped pay for everything. She was the mother that Flip never had; her abandonment of the family triggering a psychological entertainment response in him as a coping mechanism for the lossful pain the rest of his life. Geraldine was a stylish and self assured, financially secure woman who never cheated on her Killer, had strong principles based in self respect, homespun old school values, a flirtatious sense of humor, and dance moves. Her biggest crossover appeal was not to the white audience, but to the mass female audience. That rare and supremely commercially powerful demographic that rules 55% of the earth. Geraldine on NBC had a topline budget for designer European outfits, purses, and shoes including bright, attention grabbing threads by Emilio Pucci, thanks to Joyce Moore's connect in Miami. Bam. The psychology of visual communication. Geraldine wasn't wearing secondhand clothes, domestic workwear, or church clothes. It was expensive European fabrics and shoes. America was took by storm. The main thing to get there was stage time. Confidence. Studying as many different audiences against as many different stories, characters, words, and expressions as Flip could think of or be influenced by in the real world. You heard of Porky's, right? World famous party bar in Ft Lauderdale they named those classic comedy movies after in the 80s. Flip Wilson played there in 1957 (A year ahead of George Kirby). When he really wasn't nobody. And the ad in the Ft Lauderdale News said, "Rock 'N' Roll Show Tonite 10p.m. - Four Big Miami Acts - Candy Williams, Fluffy Smith, Nip 'N' Tuck, and Flip Wilson - Comedian. Porky's Show Bar. 3900 N. Federal Hwy. No minors." Place was crawling with pesky damn high school kids every weekend. Bar was wild. Had a big old barbecue restaurant. They had a killer jazz jam, "all colored" nights, rock and roll shows with black artists from the Miami clubs. Had Calypso Eddie every Tuesday night direct from Vegas and everything. What a dive. Three hundred cap. Big, open air, screened in dance floor. Used to have "Ft Lauderdale's only 4 piece colored dance band." Their one year anniversary was 1957, and they had free beer and free hot dogs for everybody. Broward County in 1957 had a strong black history, but was a white power dominated county named after a confederate who became Governor of Florida, Napoleon Bonaparte Broward. Half the families never got word that the Civil War was over, and don't dare tell em' who won. But

dammit if those long-white-dress and mask
wearing crossburners didn't love that funny
talking black lady just the same.

Flip Wilson was funny, man.

INFO. 374-2444

Tickets Available: Sid's, East & West, Ft. Lauderdale; Record Land, Hollywood, 163rd St.; Tapesville, Miracle Mile & Hialeah; Records Unlimited, Red Road, South Miami; Rock of Ages, Boca Raton; Jeans, Etc., West Palm Beach; Gusman Box Office, Flagler St.

Service Charge at All Outlets

GEORGE CARLIN

George Carlin got high with Flip Wilson and Richard Pryor backstage of a tv gig, and after that he got funnier. Up until then, he was sort of a square cat.

Flip always had good weed and pure cocaine, and they partook the goods backstage of the Kraft Comedy Special, a cheese-sponsored TV variety hour, and it set all of their careers in a new direction. Flip told the two young comics to come from the heart, cut it with the canned-laugh-material, find what's funny in something real and take it to the stage. A couple of years later, he hired them as staff writers on his TV show.

Intelligent stupidity. Witty urbane social satire. Semantic disassembly, frank discussions on sex and sexuality, political ribbing, interrogating race relations, drug-infused, popular subversion, youthful, lustful, consumerist, and media conscious comedy is what the Playboy Clubs sought to proliferate their image through via the comics in their clubs. Playboy Club gave young George Carlin his early legs in the game, alonside his comedy partner, and they called themselves Carlin and Burns, even if they mostly bombed. Hugh Heffner's international network of sexy lounges with hot bunnies had the power to book hip comics into their many outposts at a time. George Carlin was traveling with his young bride Brenda, who he'd just married, and his comedy partner, a guy named Jack Burns. They had the good fortune to lock into a nationwide tour. The Miami Playboy Club was located at 7701 Biscayne Boulevard. If you need a frame of reference, 79th and Biscayne is one of the most active blocks in the City of Miami and it has been since the beginning. The original Coppertone billboard is around there, and so is Sun Gym from the movie Pain & Gain. The immigration office was there for a long time, and it's sort of always been a pickup track for tricks on the block, liquor, reefer, cocaine, heroin, crack, slums, clearance, renewal, and gentrification. Old school neon light motels from the 1950's are getting knocked over for high rises, but some of them are still there. The Sinbad, the Shalimar, the New Yorker. Funny tubs and heart shaped beds in rooms with mirrored ceilings, and seventy five years worth of cum soaked sheets. Carlin was staying at one of them with his new wife. Blasting some of the first loads in those rooms, no doubt. They were living next door to the Playboy Club in a crummy motel.

Miami Herald
June 13, 1961

Playboy Club - Singer Johnny Janis, songstress Pepi Runnels, the comedy team of Jack Burns and George Carlin, Balladier guitarist Stan Wilson and comedy impersonator Adam Keefe.

Not exactly an a-list lineup, but hey, it was the middle of the summer, ninety two degrees and rainy. In the winter it would be slamming, for Carlin and Burns it was at least a job.

Then Carlin's mom and aunt called and said they were coming down for a girl's trip. On his honeymoon for gosh sakes. It would be years and years before George Carlin dropped acid and got hip to new ways of thinking. How to freak the masses.

His comedy throughout most of the 1960s was safe. Conventional. Establishment. But, don't get it confused. He was a professional touring standup comic living a life of adventure on the streets of America. In the clubs every night in all of the biggest cities, getting chased out of small towns. You name it. But his set was clean as a whistle dipped in bleach. Clever, silly, expressive, emotive, hyperactive, and talented, sure; unaware of comedy's seismic shifting social power, to hold a crowd accountable, in rapture, and program new ideas while making them laugh.

Soon he'd strike fear into the heart of the FCC for his comedic vocabulary, but on November 2, 1968, he served as the, "Piece de resistance of the evening," said the Miami Herald, "At a very posh bash thrown at the Four Ambassadors, for the Greater Miami Radio Broadcasters Association." Nice check for a corporate gig no doubt. Just funny for the comic who would soon immortalize a bit on seven dirty words: "Shit, piss, fuck, cunt, cocksucker, motherfucker, and tits," to collect that commercial broadcast radio industry money. Hilarious.

In 1976, Carlin played a solo concert at Dade County Auditorium. In 1977, he did the Gusman Hall. In 1978, he headlined the Sunrise Musical Theater for John Lomelo. Carlin worked the system and then made a fool of it. Class clown.

CELLAR DOOR CONCERTS

presents

SATURDAY — NOV. 1st

2 SHOWS: 8:30 pm & MIDNIGHT

MIAMI JAI ALAI

"RICHARD PRYOR"

WITH SPECIAL GUEST

"TAVARES"

PLUS

"STREET CORNER SYMPHONY"

AVAILABLE AT:

Sid's East and West of Ft. Lauderdale; Record Shack, 163rd St.; Keetie's Westchester, all Teds Hip Shops; Big Ben's, Northside Shop Ctr., Rudy's Record's and Tapes Miami; Chucks Records & Tapes, Hollywood; Rodgers Sound in Perrine

RICHARD PRYOR

Richard Pryor. He made crowds uncomfortable; with laughter. Cutting edge, controversial, lighting up the stage, the screen, the airwaves, albums, and the streets. His career was on fire. And in five years, he would be too. But in 1975, he was hot. So hot that Saturday Night Live had to have him. It was their first season. Episode seven. Pryor would be the first black host. Lorne Michaels was a fan. NBC was in. Nervously. The year of 1975 was coming to a close. The Vietnam War was over. "Love Will Keep Us Together" by Captain and Tenille was the year's number one song. Stephen King ruled the book charts with Salem's Lot. JAWS was the number one movie. Popular culture was rife with material for to satire. Richard Pryor was eight albums deep, between his authorized and bootleg Laff releases, and he had more to say than ever. SNL was a big stage, Pryor's favorite kind. But he had demands, and paranoias, and comic mischief, erratic, ironic, uncontrolled, delusional, maniacal, and incisive, incongruous perspective and speech. Funny. Which is exactly what Lorne Michaels said he'd better be. Under his breath. His jaw was wired and tight. They both were, for different reasons. Pryor told Lorne to fly the NBC Jet with a team full of suits to talk it out with him backstage at his headline show at the Miami Jai Alai, home of the fastest sport on earth. Each side brought their proverbial cestas, the wicker basket that players used to launch the jai alai pelota at 188 miles per hour. Talk about high-powered negotiations. Richard Pryor was high as a kite. He had the best rock, the best powder, liquor, reefer, hash, acid, shrooms, horse, ludes, vals, dust… whatever he needed or wanted. Lorne kept it cool, few drinks, a little of this or that, whatever, but some of the execs were cutting loose at the hottest show in the city. There were freaks and booze and blow aplenty at Miami Jai Alai. 36th street and northwest 37th Avenue. Big parking lot. Close to the old Florida East Coast railroad tracks, Miami International Airport, the 95, the 836, the Okeechobee Trail. A crossroads of good and evil at the exchange of life and money. With death's cold stairs on every corner. Strip clubs and the river and the warehouses. There were chop shops, fuck shops, and stash spots, and guns, and boats, and ammo all around. Strange times were afoot. The CIA, The FBI, thc early wave cartel narcos, the Sandinistas, the military juntas, they all partied the same places at this time. With regularity at the Jai Alai which was a well known open air drug market of sorts, at the time, at least in the sense of how many deals were cut there, with gambling excitement and live entertainment as the action packed backdrop. The Richard

Pryor element invigorated the city, the whole Miami-Dade County, with a fervent working class party funk. All nations under the flying freak flag of comedy with Pryor leading the charge, and a 6,500 capacity arena crowd; and the Jai Alai floating on an ocean of reefer smoke. All the players had a spoon. All the ladies were looking for a vial. The cops were high. The security were high. The halter top and bell bottom cuties with the fat booties and the big dick machos with their hands on their balls were feeling good. The crowd's fully-charged laugh-batteries were ready to burst. You could smell the ether in the air. Cut with anbesol. Festival time. Draft beer, buttered popcorn, vomit. An army of laughers ready to bust. Pryor had the power. The leverage. So he forced the issue with Lorne and the suits. He would do the show, but he had conditions. Paul Mooney had to be head writer. His buddy Thalmus needed to be in as an actor. Pryor's ex-wife and new girlfriend each had to get a monologue. Gil Scott-Heron had to do the music, televising his personal revolution through a song called "Johannesburg" going against apartheid in South Africa. Final point, he needed over half the tickets to the studio audience so he could flood it with his people. Rich wanted in on every aspect of the production, manufacturing, distribution. He would be good. He promised. He would do as he was told and everything would go great. He would portray a janitor in a sketch written by Paul Mooney. He would let Chevy Chase call him “Nigger.” He would call Chase a “A Dead Honky!” Funny stuff. This was America prosecuting itself, exposing broadcast airtime and the burning heat of the spotlights to the festering wound of the birth of the nation to its original sin; cauterizing that rotten festered wound through the absolution of purifying comedy. The deal was worked out over the boozy dream of a backstage meeting at an indoor arena in Miami.

NOW—MIAMI BEACH OFFICE
FOR ROOM RESERVATIONS
PHONE (305) 673-1551

Opens Wednesday, Feb. 16

DON RICKLES

MARILYN MICHAELS

Coming March 15

TOTIE FIELDS

VIC DAMONE

DON RICKLES

Don Rickles. Insult comic. Tough guy. Jew. He fired a machine gun from a rubber bubbler for the U.S. Navy during World War II. Born in Jackson Heights, Queens, New York City. Son of an insurance salesman and a mountain lion. Single child. Frank Sinatra called him Bullethead. He had a head like a bullet, a geschlumpfka face, and a crazy look in his eye that said, "Let's go, what are *you* gonna do." But the funniest thing about Rickles, he was a mama's boy to a comedy stage-mom who used to go to all his early shows and tell him "Oh, Don, but do you have to be so mean?!" In the early days, she followed him everywhere. His manager. Momager. Momma Womanager. And he loved having her. It was 1956. They were living on Miami Beach. He had a little place, and she split an apartment with a friend of hers, another New York Jew broad whose husband had died like hers. RIP Max Rickles, who would be proud. His kid was playing Murray Franklin's. A twenty-five seat joint with a hot late show. Small place. If someone farted everybody smelled it. Herb Kelly from the Miami News described it as a, "Padded cell with a liquor license," and, "An asylum for insomniacs." Had all kind of funny decorations. Souvenir plates from famous prisons. Sing Sing. San Quentin. Alcatraz.

Had a sign that said, "Se Habla Yiddish." Hand lettered sign out front that said, "Audience wanted. No experience necessary." Best of all, the seats in the show-room were rocking chairs. That was the gimmick. Rocking chairs. Cause Murray Franklin figured comfortable seats would keep people in the place. And at first everybody thought he was crazy. An Irish-Jew, "Lepre-Cohen" from New York City, according to Herby Kelly, who "Ran bars, dives, and cesspools" for twenty-five years before opening his own place in MB, where he got to do everything his way. Buxom blondes at the bar. Singing cocktail waitress, and singing cooks. Show time was all the time and everybody was part of the show if they worked there or not. Murray played a guitar made from a stick and a bedpan and he ribbed the crowd. Got everyone involved. Had a long cord on the microphone and went all over. Used to sit down and drink and talk from the tables. Things started to happen. The place filled up. Line to get in. Crowd outside smoking, drinking, cutting up. By 1956, Herb Rau from the Miami Herald said, "You have to make a reservation for a rocking chair." The club was across from Roney Plaza. Fancy schmancy. Franklin's place stayed open to 5a.m. Early morning is when his offbeat humor and fan interactions clicked. He found a big-band song-milf named Roberta Sherwood, stuck her in the spotlight, and let her big voice ring. She was 43 years old and had hospital bills for her husband; and three teenage sons to care for. Her showbiz prospects had faded but she had power. Herb Rau from the Miami Herald mentioned her in an article. Then her old pal Red Buttons, the comedian, came in and saw her. Buttons told Walter Winchell, America's biggest columnist. Winchell caught the act and wrote her up and it went to papers around the country. He was a one man gossip wire service. Thanks to the attention, she got a twelve record deal with Decca, an appearance on the Jackie Gleason show, a headline slot at the Pompeii Room in the Eden Roc Hotel, gigs around the country, platinum off a jukebox. She and her three sons appeared on the Lucille Ball show. After that, nobody could shut Murray Franklin up. He thought he was Ed Sullivan. The king of talent. Everybody started saying he was crazy again. And then he booked a young comedian nobody ever heard of called Don Rickles. A few spaghetti forking meatballs from Brooklyn knew him from the Elegante room up there in New York, but Rickles was a drama school wannabe whose only notoriety up to that point was a glass-skull bit that he had a hit with in Detroit and Washington D.C., depicting a man whose every thought is plainly visible to everyone through his transparent head, and how it drives him crazy. He built the bit at strip clubs, back when they featured comedians who had to fight for attention. Matter of fact, Lenny Bruce's mom Sally Marr was stripping at the club in D.C. where Rickles did the glass bit. But something changed in him when he got to Miami Beach. It was like he himself was the glass skull all along. He started saying everything that was on his mind about everyone around him. Capturing a moment of recognition, reducing everyone to whatever funny, ugly thing about them stuck out. Double punching their guts for maximum insult. Don Rickles, the acerbic riffer on whatever face he was faced with. It was a nightly battle between his id and his lid, boiling over with hilarity anywhere that would let him on stage.

August 1956. Herb Rau. Miami Herald. Don Rickles, "Visiting showpeople catch the brunt of the guys' insults - but he throws a curve or two at anybody who happens to be around ringside or at the bar." Anyone. Any time. On sight. He was throwing ego-smashers at celebrities, at tourists, at bartenders, club owners. Even Jackie Gleason, the Great One himself stumbled in to Murray Franklin's one night, drunk as an eight armed sailor, got up on the stage and told Rickles to say something funny. Rickles was building a rep for his confrontational style that's for sure. Reviewers talked about his attacks on people's religions, nationalities, and personal appearance to packed rooms. He targeted himself too. He made so many jokes about Jews, that the Jews were scared of him. He had a schtick. All he needed was the right target. That's where Etta Rickles came in. Don's mom. She was ready. Etta treated Miami Beach like New York's fifth borough. She knew every bingo caller, shuffleboard hustler, and matzah ball slinger on Collins and Washington Aves, and all the double hanger floozies sitting on the hotel porches on Ocean Drive. She knew all the cops on 11th, all the bookies on 12th, and the best place for Chinese on 14th. It was the yenta network, a fast-talking information system in the language of the streets. The beach was full of Jews, Italians, and Irish. It felt like Queens. Etta fit right in. So when her roommate's butcher's cousin's uncle's wife told her that Frank Sinatra's mom was in town at the Fontainebleau Hotel, she knew she had a chance to get Frank Sinatra to her Don. On a sunny day in a Fontainebleau cabana, between the glimmering Atlantic and the lively resort pool, Etta sent two white doves, a seafood tower, two passes for the spa, and a manila envelope full of green faces, and next thing you know Frank Sinatra, the big shot himself, was walking into little Murray Franklin's. Now this may sound exaggerated, it is, but it's basically true. I made up the doves and the seafood tower, but Dolly Sinatra and Etta Rickles did meet up at the Fontainebleau, become friends for life, and Frank showed up to Murray Franklin's and met Rickles there. Decades later, Sinatra still recalled how the mom's got along. When Rickles saw Sinatra walk into the club, he called out through the mic, "Oh look who it is. Frank Sinatra. Make yourself comfortable, Frank. Hit Somebody!" Frank Sinatra was a mob-connected tough-guy with a trail of crimson footprints where those borne aloft on the wings of his enmity were crushed under his cronies union boots. Comedian Jackie Mason found out all about this the hard way when he was beaten on the streets of Miami Beach by Sinatra's thug pals in 1967. Losers found themselves on the wrong ends of his fists on the regular. Don's joke had Sinatra howling and all his goons too. The club was watching the star and before you know it, little Murray Franklin's was shaking to the low ceiling with explosive laughter between amplified outbursts of concentrated vitriol as Rickles kept tagging his joke. Fake venom, for as Etta, Frank, and Dolly Sinatra already knew, Don Rickles was a nice Jewish momma's boy. Now he had a voice and a confidence. In 1957, Lenny Bruce got kicked off the opening night of a new club in L.A. and the Slate Brothers who owned the place heard of Rickle's rep and had him replace Lenny. The Slate Brothers were connected to the movie business so a steady stream of showbiz people came through, and that's where Rickles got practice ripping on a room full of famous people night after night. He came back to Miami even stronger. Miami Herald. November 20, 1957. "Don Rickles, who will have his own club in the former Chez Paree on Miami Beach next month, has a role in "Run Silent, Run Deep," starring Clark Gable and Burt Lancaster." The LA run had paid off big time. He got noticed by Hollywood and now he was in a big movie. Then he got his own comedy room, The Riot Room, in a hotel on Liberty Ave. His picture was in the Miami Herald in a bold advertisement with his vicious smile evoking raucous laughter. His name was ringing in the streets. In 1958, State Attorney Richard E. Gerstein, who later prosecuted the Watergate scandal, and eventually represented Pee Wee Herman for indecent exposure, and still has a justice building in Miami named after him, had Rickles come in as a "special investigator" to make fun of everybody on his staff. Rickles up there making fun of Jew lawyers, and Puerto Rican criminals, and the Cuban "monster show" in Havana, where a guy with a thirteen-incher went to town on some cousin of theirs from Poughkeepsie. It was a hilarious gig in the long line of cops, firemen, and corporates that comics still work today. But then Rickles got caught slipping. 1958. The Matador Room at the Seville Hotel. Bombing. The opposite of laughs. Groans, and worse, silence. Rich white ladies all offended. Complaints to the manager. Bad reviews. James Bacon. Associated Press. "Rickles. He flopped." Out for everyone to read on the national wire! People walked out. He was overdoing it. Had to learn to pull back. How to deliver mean while keeping it nice and friendly. The ironic highwire of his whole act. Next stop Biscayne Boulevard. December 1958. The Admiral Vee. 80th and Biscayne. Biscayne being US1. That good old American highway connecting Miami to New York City, the lifeblood of Rickles' brash, aggressive style. This was his first big testing grounds in the City of Miami, fewer tourists than the beach, and the wrong word could get him killed. But instead of getting whacked, it was the other way around. Rickles killed the audience every night. The very people he was making fun of were his biggest fans. His face was in the paper opposite Sophie Tucker at Latin Quarter. The review was in. Herb Rau. January 2, 1959. Headline: "Rickles Cuts Up At Admiral Vee." He'd become himself. The Mad Emperor of insult comedy was ready for the big time.

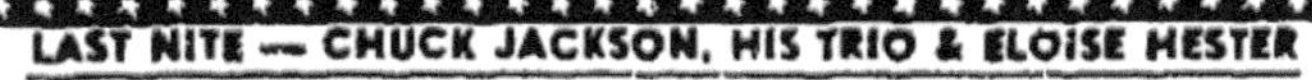
LAST NITE — CHUCK JACKSON, HIS TRIO & ELOISE HESTER
Next Weekend—Recording Star REDD FOXX, Comedian

CLYDE KILLEN'S
SIR JOHN HOTEL
KNIGHT BEAT

REDD FOXX

THE BIGGEST SALES ARE ON DOOTO!!!

HATTIE NOEL

NEW RED HOT RECORDS

Tops in Recorded Entertainment

Fabulous and spectacular recordings by the top Negro artists recorded at their best.
A catalog of world-wide appeal spanning the musical spectrum from exciting jazz to inspiring vocals and hilarious comedy performed by top talent.
Recorded in high fidelity sound to please the most discriminating.

REDD FOXX

NEW RELEASES

Dooto's newest, sidesplitting funmaker, Top party LP. DTL 825 $4.98

Billy Allyn, Funnier than Foxx. A guaranteed party riot. DTL 826 $4.98

Another Redd Foxx Smash!

Favorite TV and Radio jokes, Parking Ticket and others. DTL 234 $4.98

Gene & Freddie, Hilarious take-off on TV show "Night Court." DTL 827 $4.98

Foxx's funniest best seller, includes Earth Quake, Pregnancy, etc. DTL 275 $4.98

CURRENT BEST SELLERS

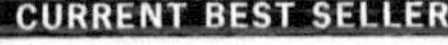

Smash Laughs, Red Riding Hood, Shave Your Hair. DTL 820 $4.98

Great Negro Gospel Singers. The Blood, The Spirit. DTL 807 $3.98

Hilarious, Puppy Pants, Blowing Bubbles, Cutting, etc. DTL 824 $4.98

A Scream, The Second Hole, The Razor Blade, etc. DTL 823 $4.98

Risque songs by Hattie Noel & Billy Mitchell. DTL 212 $4.98

Redd Foxx, Two Oars, Brown Nosed Reindeer, etc. DTL 219 $4.98

Redd Foxx, Turned to Stone, Dead Jackass, Guided Muscle. DTL 220 $4.98

Redd Foxx, Soldier & Sailor, Crosseyed Rooster, Wise Crack. DTL 227 $4.98

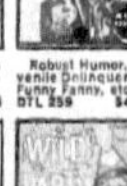

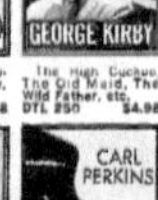

Hysterical Jokes, Lickedysplit, Shooting Craps, etc. DTL 253 $4.98

The Letter, Buick 59, Heaven and Paradise, Mind Go Wild. DTL 204 $3.98

Robust Humor, Juvenile Delinquency, Funny Fanny, etc. DTL 259 $4.98

The High Cuckoo, The Old Maid, The Wild Father, etc. DTL 250 $4.98

Redd Foxx, Exploded Roach, Plugged In, Trombone Playing. DTL 236 $4.98

Redd Foxx, Includes Feeling Low Down, Stinking Fork, etc. DTL 265 $4.98

Sloppy Daniels, Kathy Cooper & Skillet, etc. DTL 266 $4.98

Redd Foxx, Rendition contains Tarzan, Mother Frockers, etc. DTL 270 $4.98

Burlesque Hilarity, The Bad Dream and others. DTL 232 $4.98

Hot Tales, The Mother, The Brassiere, Sister's Dress. DTL 801 $4.98

Hotel Talk, The Congo Cannibal, The Indian & Spook, etc. DTL 804 $4.98

Jazz by Carl Perkins, Way Cross Town, Carl's Blues, etc. DTL 211 $3.98

World War II, Slow To Come, Pajama Sex, Pregnant Ballerina. DTL 290 $4.98

Redd Foxx, Selected gems of clean humor for entire family. DTL 01 $4.98

Chuck Higgins, Roy Milton, Wetback Hop, Tonky Honk, Oh Yeah. DTL 223 $3.98

Baron Harris, Includes Sexy Dan, Snow White, etc. DTL 294 $4.98

Medallions, Penguins, Cuffinks, etc. So Tough, Be A Fool. DTL 501 $3.98

Top Comics, Redd Foxx, George Kirby, Sloppy Daniels, etc. DTL 274 $4.98

Best Selling Album, Race Track, New Soap, The Jackass. DTL 214 $4.98

Holy Golf Game, Licked Husband, The Big Possee, etc. DTL 295 $4.98

Lillian Randolph Singers, Room Enuf, Were You There, etc. DTL 221 $3.98

Redd Foxx, Sleeping Deacon, Missionary Manu, Breast Bed. DTL 815 $4.98

Spicy Stories, gags and jokes. The 24" Zipper, The GI, etc. DTL 814 $4.98

Hits by Meadowlarks, Pipes, Romancers, Penguins, etc. DTL 224 $3.98

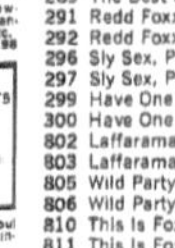

Hilarious Haymaker which will cause convulsive laughter. DTL 808 $4.98

All-time top vocal group, Didie-goodie hits by the Penguins. DTL 242 $3.98

Designed by the Comedy King to fill parties with fun. DTL 809 $4.98

Buddy Collette, Quintet featured in best contemp jazz. DTL 245 $3.98

Redd Foxx, Shooting the Rear, Pajama Tops, Black Sheep. DTL 298 $4.98

Dexter Gordon Blows Hot, Carl Perkins, and others. DTL 207 $3.98

Don Bexley and Dave Turner, The Heckler, and others. DTL 238 $4.98

Zion Travelers, Soul Revivers, Vitalized, inspiring, religious. DTL 225 $3.98

Blame It On The Blues, Everybody Has A Fool, other hits. DTL 293 $3.98

Redd Foxx, The Hollywood Playboy, The Plastic Surgery. DTL 249 $4.98

Gene & Freddy, Naughty & crazy, Superman's Balls, etc. DTL 279 $4.98

ORDER TODAY from this select list of DOOTO RECORDS best sellers!

SINGLES 45 RPM only $ .99

BILLY MITCHELL
101 Song Of The Woodpecker
110 Willie Sure Could Do It
REDD FOXX
385 The New Soap
390 The Jackasses
397 The Honeymooners
402 Beans and Pineapple Juice
408 The Two Oars
411 The Dead Jackass
416 Fun In The Crazy House
418 Best Of Foxx
421 The House
426 Hollywood Playboy
453 Dear John Letter
455 The Shoe Shine Boy
458 118 Ways
460 Come Kitty
464 Xmas Hard Times
CHAS. McCULLOUGH & THE SILKS
462 My Girl
465 You're Not Too Young
467 I Cried All Night
EDDIE SILVERS & ORCHESTRA
468 The Party Rocker

SLOPPY DANIELS
415 The Bad Dream
447 Three And Four Times
449 The Baby Maker
450 The Tent Pole
DON BEXLEY & DAVE TURNER
420 The Virgin
431 The Golf Game
HATTIE NOEL
461 My Passionate Man
THE PENGUINS
348 Earth Angel
353 Ookey Ook
VERNON GREEN & MEDALLIONS
347 Buick '59
364 Edna
446 Magic Mountain
DON JULIAN & THE MEADOWLARKS
359 Heaven & Paradise
367 Always & Always
372 This Must Be Paradise
THE CUFF LINKS
409 Guided Missiles
422 It's Too Late Now
433 So Tough

THE FINEST NEGRO ENTERTAINMENT

DOOTO RECORDS
9512 SO. CENTRAL AVE. • LOS ANGELES 2, CAL.

ORDER THESE HARD-TO-GET EXTENDED PLAY ALBUMS TODAY!

EP 45 RPM $1.29

202 The Medallions
203 Don Julian & The Meadowlarks
206 Helen Humes Sings & Swings
208 Rhythm, Rock and Roll
— The Penguins
201 The Penguins
241 The Cool, Cool Penguins, Pt. 1
243 The Cool, Cool Penguins, Pt. 2
244 The Cool, Cool Penguins, Pt. 3
— Carl Perkins
213 Modern Jazz Stylings

EP 45 RPM $1.49

— Billy Mitchell
210 Party Songs For Grownups
— Redd Foxx
215 Laff Of The Party, Vol. 1
217 Laff Of The Party, Vol. 2
218 Laff Of The Party, Vol. 3
222 Laff Of The Party, Vol. 4
228 Laff Of The Party, Vol. 5
230 Best Of Foxx, Vol. 1, Pt. 1
231 Laff Of The Party, Vol. 7
233 Best Of Foxx, Vol. 1, Pt. 2
235 Laff Of The Party, Vol. 7
237 Burlesque Humor, Pt. 2
254 The Sidesplitter, Pt. 1
255 The Sidesplitter, Pt. 2
256 The Sidesplitter, Pt. 3
263 Laff Of The Party, Vol. 8, Pt. 1
264 Laff Of The Party, Vol. 8, Pt. 2
271 The Sidesplitter, Vol. 2, Pt. 1
272 The Sidesplitter, Vol. 2, Pt. 2
273 The Sidesplitter, Vol. 2, Pt. 3
276 Racy Tales, Pt. 1
277 Racy Tales, Pt. 2
278 Racy Tales, Pt. 3
286 Best Party Fun, Pt. 1
287 Best Party Fun, Pt. 2
288 The Best Laff, Pt. 1
289 The Best Laff, Pt. 2
291 Redd Foxx Funn, Pt. 1
292 Redd Foxx Funn, Pt. 2
296 Sly Sex, Pt. 1
297 Sly Sex, Pt. 1
299 Have One On Me, Pt. 1
300 Have One On Me, Pt. 2
802 Laffarama, Pt. 1
803 Laffarama, Pt. 2
805 Wild Party, Pt. 1
806 Wild Party, Pt. 2
810 This Is Foxx, Pt. 1
811 This Is Foxx, Pt. 2
816 He's Funny That Way, Pt. 1
817 He's Funny That Way, Pt. 2
821 Foxx At Jazzville, Pt. 1
822 Foxx At Jazzville, Pt. 2
— Hattie Noel
216 House Party Songs
— Sloppy Daniels
229 Laff Of The Party, Vol. 6
267 Sloppy's House Party, Pt. 1
268 Sloppy's House Party, Pt. 2
269 Sloppy's House Party, Pt. 3
— Bexley & Turner
239 Laff Of The Party
— George Kirby
257 Night In Hollywood
258 Night In Hollywood
— Allen Drew
260 Stag Party, Pt. 1
261 Stag Party, Pt. 2
262 Stag Party, Pt. 3
— Gene & Freddie
280 Party Record, Pt. 1
281 Party Record, Pt. 2
282 Party Record, Pt. 3
— Scatman Crothers
818 Comedy Sweepstakes, Pt. 1
819 Comedy Sweepstakes, Pt. 2

REDD FOXX

Redd Foxx invented party records. Him and Walter "Dootsie" Williams. They were the first. One standup comic, on a mic, in front of a live, public, nightclub audience, recorded, mixed, mastered, pressed up, shipped out, and sold nationally.

The album used clips from different shows crudely cut as bits in the form of jump cuts that sold-through fast, made millions of bucks and initiated a hyperactive catalog.

Redd Foxx loved cocaine, reefer, cigarettes and alcohol, broads, festivities, nightclubs, and standup comedy. He died of a heart attack while on set of his 1991, Eddie Murphy backed tv show. He was being interviewed for a segment of Lifestyles Of The Rich And Famous when some dumbass network bitch cut in on the production trying to tell him what to do. On his own show. It was too much for any man, but hey, what a run.

Redd Foxx. 1956. Laff Of The Party vol. 1. Dootone Records. The first true standup comedy album. One comic voice in a live set. Not George Kirby or Mort Sahl. Not Goodman and Buchanan and their Flying Saucer. Not Milton Berle, or Jack Benny, or

George Jefferson. It was John Sanford aka Chicago Red. And when Dootsie Williams first offered him a record deal, he said no. Then the next day he took $25 to do it cause he needed the money. Redd Foxx Laff Of The Party Vol. 1 became the biggest comedy album of all time for quite a while, selling a million copies rather unexpectedly for all parties. It's got everything. Foxx even farts into the mic. Sure there had been novelty records, musical comedy, parody, satire, and even jokes on wax going all the way back to the cylinder days, but standup comedy was a new art form that subtracted all but the singular voice from the tradition of various cultures of musical dinner theater. Dootsie Williams was an LA entrepreneur who made a boatload of cash off his writing, recording, and publishing of "Earth Angel" by The Penguins in 1954. People say that Dootsie heard Redd Foxx on stage at the Brass Rail in South Central LA, but it could have been the Club Oasis and the next day, signed the line to record him live and that's how it came about. The first volume dropped in 1956, and by 1957 there were seven volumes of Laff Of The Party and Dootone Records was advertising its catalog in Billboard. This was a far different tactic from Belle Barth's original label After Hours. Dootone was in the three major trades: Billboard, Cashbox, and Record World. It had an address, a backstory, wholesale pricing, inventory, an order form, and contact info. Surprise and After Hours labels hid everything. Thanks to the pioneering doo wop track, "Earth Angel," an independent hit, Dootsie had infrastructure, capital, pressing plants able to meet popular demand on a credit line, and distribution. Comedy was easier to record and produce, relatively speaking, with fewer moving parts to deal with overall than a band or musician. With a good engineer it could sound amazing. With just about anybody pushing the record button, it might be good enough to be a hit. So Dooto, which the label name shortened to, became prolific in its output. The label dropped albums like rabbits make bunnies, rapidly generating a large catalog of new jokes and compilations.

By 1963, Foxx had "17 smash party records" and he was headlining for club promoter Clyde "Glass" Killens at the Sir John Hotel Knight Beat in Miami, Florida's Overtown. "Comedian Extraordinary" is what they called him and the show was three nights only, with free tables. Friday night admission cost was $2. C'mon, man. Redd Foxx Overtown for $2, what a deal. The Sir John, they probably gave him a room to be staying there as they did most artists. The compound, which included a 535 address and a 276 address held 24 hours of live music. There was a night club, a jazz lounge; hourly, nightly, weekly, and monthly rooms for rent (if you know what I mean), a pool, a bar at each of those, a 6a.m. show, and national headliners every week with a lot of them staying right there. It was a party. Foxx loved cocaine, reefer, cigarettes, broads, alcohol, festivities, nightclubs, and standup comedy. Repetition for emphasis. Hard to know who was there or what went on, but logic has it that he was sniffin', smokin', drinkin', fuckin', laughin', and making people laugh. Other performers the week Foxx played the Knight Beat were Patti LaBelle and The Blue Belles, Little Esther, and Marv Johnson.

In 1972, he was at the Marco Polo Hyatt House on the ocean at 192 street and Collins Ave, in the Persian Room. 1973, he brought down the Redd Foxx Revue. But 1974, he came back with a vengeance. With an old juke-joint routine cleaned up for the modern era. Redd was at the Fontainebleau. Sold out shows for ol' double x. Reason he was there according to Miami News was he was replacing Bill Cosby, whose show wasn't selling any tickets. Apparently the crowd was sleeping on him. Foxx charged up the atmosphere. Big ads with his name and face in all the papers. Reviews and promotional articles before, during, and after. Foxx had a trick up his shorts. After his forty minutes or an hour on stage he'd slink off, then while the band was setting up, the lights would go out, a strobe would hit, and Foxx would run out wearing flesh color tights, looking naked and helicoptering a big fat fake dick between his legs. Say he even slapped a couple guys and their old ladies in the face with it on the way across the floor (joking). Streaking was a cultural phenomenon with students at the time on university campuses throughout the U.S. running naked for any reason was in. In the comedy world it's always been there. The version Redd was doing, the strobe light dildo routine, Rudy Ray Moore did too in California. But it came from way back. They would do it in the Mississippi juke joints ass naked. Little old backwood whorehouses in Arkansas too, and the late late shows of traveling carnivals as well. The dirty show. Redd Foxx may have picked it up anywhere from St Louis to Philly, New York, Chicago, or any of the comedy shows from Alaska, to Montana, to Alabama where he started out touring. It's a gimmick going all the way back to whores and pimps. For him to do that at the Fontainebleau is hilarious. A disrespectation in permutation to the situation. "Don't leave lest you miss Redd's ultimate streak at the end of the show," said Miami News.

Foxx must have thought that was pretty funny. He was blowing off steam. This was the time when he stopped showing up for tapings of his hit show Sanford And Son with a list of grievances and demands to the NBC network before he would return. Among the problems he cited were windowless work rooms, seven day work weeks, micro managing administrators, no privacy, hack writers with stupid premises. Money, what money? He didn't wanna die on no fucking tv set, which he did, aggravated into cardiac arrest by somebody who was nobody trying to tell him what to do. Which is kind of funny, or at least cosmically ironic. Somewhat like his whole career. A pioneer since the beginning. A revolutionary like his friend Detroit Red aka Malcolm X. Either one could have gone the way of the other. Party platform. Party records. Records. Records. Redd Foxx did it first. He loved Miami because he loved to have fun. He was the laff of the party.

PRESENTS A
Barry Sinco Production
STARRING THE ONE AND ONLY

SLAPPY WHITE

COMEDIAN

Held Over For 2nd Smash Week

ALSO

EXTRA! WEEKEND ATTRACTION

MISS PHYLLIS BRANCH

Song Stylist Extraordinary

COMING JANUARY 22nd FOR ONE WEEK

JOE WILLIAMS

FORMERLY WITH COUNT BASIE

3 shows nightly starting at 10:30—Admission but no table charge
For reservations: Call Charles — 36th St. Exway to 27th Ave.
4200 N.W. 27th Avenue NEwton 3-0611

Hampton House

CLUB

Direct from Ed Sullivan
& Jack Paar

SLAPPY WHITE

3
SHOWS
NITELY

Opening
Jan. 22nd
JOE
WILLIAMS

4200 N.W. 27th AVE.
PHONE NE 3-0611
Take 36th St. Expressway to 27th Ave.

SLAPPY WHITE

Slappy White ran off with a traveling carnival at the age of 12 and made a successful life of comedy for himself, clocking a cool million bucks a year at the Flamingo in Las Vegas at his peak. He was a pioneer in mixing audiences, playing for black and white crowds throughout Miami, and probably throughout the U.S., even in the early to mid 1950s, when nobody was talking about let alone advertising that. But mainly, Slappy was a sharp and funny comedian who got started in standup as a buddy act with Redd Foxx. They hit the road for four years before he went solo on the Dinah Washington tour. Dinah Washington was Queen Of Song and she was known for highly commanding money, respect, and running through men like some women run through rumors, one, two, or three at a time. She had Slappy do material before her shows and found that he killed even though he was working clean. She hired him to open all her shows, and after four years he went full solo.

December 1955:

Now appearing. One of the vocal greats of our time. The inimitable Al Hibbler. Plus America's newest comic sensation Slappy White. Four shows nightly. Last show 3a.m.

Miami's most exciting niteclub. Club Calvert. White and colored guests welcome! N.W. 3rd Ave at 6th st.

December 1955 is the month and year that Rosa Parks refused to go to the back of the bus in Alabama, kicking off the Montgomery Bus Boycott. The nation was charged up and boiling over with racial violence, especially the south, with Florida leading the pack in many ways. And sure this book is all about comedy and comedians and laughs, but you gotta look at what was going on at the time and place that it was being created, and this is what it was. Slappy White was headlining the San Souci on Miami Beach in 1955, "The sensational young negro comedian." But he couldn't stay at that hotel. And if police caught him there at night, don't matter how light skinned he was, Slappy White would be breaking dark-after-dark laws and subject to arrest or a free meal of a knuckle sandwich, side of jail. Meanwhile, the KKK had a local office in the city, and the city had a local office in the KKK. They were buddy buddy. So running a Miami Herald ad with "whites and colored welcome" was a bold and dangerous act. Club Calvert was a protected Mafia interest, but still subject to police shakedowns, raids by Beverage Agents, weaponized code compliance inspections, and any other number of harassments, violence, and financial disruptions used to enforce the status quo. Slappy was getting money all ways, playing white crowds on the white side, mixed crowds on the black side, and side crowds in the middle. Had a head like a football player, with a jaw like a fighter. He worked clean and had a famous bit to close out where he wore a white and black glove and brought them together to make a greater point about the one united humankind. JFK gave him an award for it not long before he was murdered in Texas. The Club Calvert was not open for long, but Slappy White played it three times in three months: December 1955 with Al Hibbler, January '56 with The Inkspots, and February '56 with Dinah Washington. On February 26th, two people were arrested in a raid at the club. An underage white girl and the manager. One of the detectives then sought to get a warrant on Albert Goldman, one of the owners. The Miami Herald reported that the white girl was sitting at a table with a "negro couple," and she was charged with "being a minor loitering in a bar." The manager was charged with "selling intoxicating beverages to a minor." This may have been a case exactly as the police described in their report, or the white girl could have been an underage plant used like a pawn to justify throwing charges at the establishment. Messing with its economics. There was a well known cop, Sheriff Tom Kelly, who was said to be corrupt, who took bribes, and arranged setups on establishments in order to drum up business for his protection racket. This could have easily been related to that. R&B music's first saxophone star, Illinois Jacquet, crooner Roy Hamilton, the one and only lady Billie Holiday, piano boogieman Ivory Joe Hunter, Sister Rosetta Tharpe, LaVerne Baker, The Drifters, Louis Jordan, and Dinah Washington, and that was just about it. The Club Calvert closed in February of 1956 and Dinah Washington with Slappy White for an open audience was the last show there. In May of 1956 it reopened under a new name as the Club Basin Street.

In June of '56, just as the new club opened with new management, they got raided. "The manager of the Club Basin Street in the Miami Negro section was fined $75 in Municipal Court today for allowing minors, all of them White, on the premises," according to The Miami News. Club manager Montrose Gardner was convicted and fined after a 15 year old white girl and twenty year old white boy testified they were allowed in the club. Sounds like a setup, but hey, the racket had to get their cut off the top in order to insure that kind of thing didn't happen. The next edition of the paper carried the Club Basin Street advertisement announcing Flip Wilson as the comedy find of 1956.

March of 1957, the Club Basin Street was still going, but seemed to stop advertising after that.

The Knight Beat opened on 4th of July, 1960.

It would be years before this club was publicly announced by a third party credible source in a newspaper article as having an official policy of all audiences welcome.

Slappy White was a comedy, entertainment, and night club pioneer.

THE JOKERS are WILD!!!
January 29 - February 11
FRANK SINATRA
JOE E. LEWIS
The exciting HALF BROTHERS
Val Olman and his Orchestra
Shows: 9 and 12 nightly
No cover charge
Mr. Lewis accompanied by AUSTIN MACK
Reservations: Jean — JE 2-5426
HOTEL Eden Roc
45th & COLLINS

IN THE CAFE POMPEII WE ARE PRIVILEGED TO PRESENT
Together
KING OF CLUBS
JOE E. LEWIS
with AUSTIN MACK at the piano
QUEEN OF SONG
ELLA FITZGERALD
with The Paul Smith Trio
An Electric Pair of Dancers RAYE and ROMAN
Eden Roc
Shows 9 and 12 p.m.
Dancing to Art Freeman and His Orchestra
Open 7 Days
Reservations: Jack Class — JE 2-2451 after 2 p.m. or JE 2-2561 anytime
OPENING THURSDAY, FEBRUARY 15
GEORGE BURNS
Extra Added Attraction AL HIRT
Singing Sensation
VIVIENNE DELLA CHIESA
The Exciting Dance Styles of INGA & ROLF

JOE E. LEWIS

Singapore Sadie's, The Royal Palm, Mother Kelly's, Slapsy Maxie's, Kitty Davis, Jungle Club, The Paddock, The Nut Club, Club Bali. It was 1941. Miami Beach was the standup comedy capital of America and the world. Hundreds of nightclubs amidst the 24 hour casinos and racetracks. It was non-stop action and everybody was either in on it or trying to be. Sleep was out of the question, a tasteless act reserved for dreadful squares who existed somewhere north of the county line. The mob ruled the streets, the clubs, and the lottery. There was the Villa Venice, the Shore Club, the Shelborne, the Surfcomber, Dempsey's Sky Club, Slapsie Maxie's, Roney-Plaza, Ciro's, The Clover, The Five O'Clock, The Latin Quarter all popping, decadent, raucous, cash flush, casino rich, live act thumping Saturday night party rocking good time swing jazz, big band, rumba, salsa, and calypso dance waltzing out from the underworld, creating the sunshine state's most popular travel destination. Miami Beach. The original Vegas, which started partying during prohibition and kept saying "Hit me!" through a liquor fueled mania ruled by the lords of vice. Miami, Havana, Kingston, Port Au Prince, and Nassau formed a Caribbean Silk Road of sorts for drugs, cash, guns, liquor, sex, and banking.

At the end of the scheme was the comedian, and into their pocket went dirty bills for leading the room in entertainment, and fresh clean bills from ticket sales, food, drinks, valets, points off the broads, and smokes for the show went back in the mob's pocket. The black market infused the city's vital underworld with a nightlife flush with cash and ways to launder it. There were around 300 clubs on just that one stretch of sand according to Robert T. Fredericks, the Miami Herald's entertainment editor in July 1941, "Forty theatres in the area, 200 or 300 nightclubs, cocktail lounges, and brass railed bars…" Way before the Fontainebleau opened up in 1954. Strip joints, burlesque houses, casinos, and saloons. Restaurants with orchestras. Early shows and late shows that started at the same damn time. 5 or 6a.m. Always a party, day or night, or whatever time of artifical-burning-neon-light-emitting moment you were spinning on a rock around the sun at. Comics opened for strippers using stolen sets, paid gags, and street jokes. Hacks abounded and hounded each other for the cash grab. Got so's they'd walk into a bar just to steal jokes between their own sets. Go back to work with fresh material. Amongst those, the cream of the crop rose to the top, earning beaucoup bucks. Honorable degenerates, builders of the modern comic. Joe E. Lewis was King of the Night. America's favorite funnyman. At his court was B.S. Pully, a growling, gritty, gravel barrel of a garrulous dice rolling true blue reefer smoke and dirty gin combo with his short king of a don't call him a midget sidekick H.S. Gump. Back when comics had to fight to be heard. And they better be funny. Everyone was there for the naked chicks anyway, dig. There was women doing snake shows, in exotic outfits with feathers in funny places, teasing, and pleasing, and showcasing fire acts and wine baths, and bubbles, and limbos, and eighteen, or twenty, or thirty dancers on stages in all stages of undress. A symphony of ass. Emphasis on the G strings. There were spinning boobies, stockings, heels, and of course plenty of backroom hijinks for cold hard cash. Honey Harlow was there. Hot Honey Harlow, years before she was ever Lenny Bruce's bombshell redhead beauty, on Biscayne Boulevard at the Tropics Club, topless 17 year old working one night for a crooked house madam, the year she escaped Detroit in a sequence of stolen cars with two boys and a girlfriend, got busted for robbery and spent a year in Raiford Prison, youngest white girl in Florida history to do so at the time. There were blondes and brunettes and dolls of all shapes and sizes. They were liberated, they had money, and they liked to party. Time was fast in a hustler's market with high growth potential for committed investors. Crime was the law, and the law was enforced with a Saturday Night Special every night of the week. The joints were so down and dirty it got so you could hardly tell them apart. Especially if you were seeing double. There were men dressed like women, female impersonators being a huge business for the mob as well, homosexuality was a money maker on both sides of Miami's bridges, which were liberated from early on, with decades of ads in the Miami Herald, Miami News, and Miami Times for them right next to all the other nightclub parties. The gangsters owned the jukeboxes, the fags, the whores, the cigarette machines, the skee ball, and the pinball. It was all Mafia. The bar, the club, the performances. Maf. All the major crime families and the two-bit hustlers had rackets. All those nickels, dimes, and quarters added up. Sam Taran was a Jewish gangster from Minnesota who ended up running a lot of the jukeboxes in Florida, all those Wurlitzers and Rockolas and Seeburg's full of sounds. Entire hotels were kept in business on the bouncing backs of prostitutes timing their tricks to the beat of the jukes. So this was the atmosphere, the milieu. Gangsters, bank robbers, jewel thieves, and gamblers were the generation's anti-heros. Sophie Tucker, Joe E. Lewis, B.S. Pully, Milton Berle, Henny Youngman, Dean Martin, Myron Cohen, Desi Arnaz and Lucille Ball, were their entertainers.

There was Sophie Tucker filling another theater, showroom, radio wave (the stadium of the mind), party, club, hotel lounge, benefit, and bag of cash, fur, jewels, or sweet, sweet, hotel suite.

The charismatic pugilist of epic proportions, Slapsy Maxie owned clubs. Soon he would have two of them, "Just off both causeways, on the Miami side!," said the papers.

Another big time boxer, Joe Dempsey had been involved in the Miami nightlife for a while there too with a Sky Club, a lounge, and who knows what else. Gambling.

But the thing about Joe E. Lewis that you gotta know is his origin story, and the resilience he showed in the face of tragedy that made Frank Sinatra buy the rights to his life story to portray him in the film version of his life.

Joe E. Lewis was a young comic in the mob owned nightlife of Chicago in the 1920s. He was working under contract to a volatile twenty two year old gangster named Machine Gun Jack McGurn, to sling jokes and sing songs at his nightclub, which, ever since Joe E. Lewis built it up, was the hottest room in the city. It was so popular that another crime family offered him more money to come work for them. He agreed, told McGurn he was quitting, and Jack told him that would be a bad decision. Sure enough, one night when he was told he should expect it, McGurn's thugs busted in his room and used the butt end of a revolver to crack his skull like a rock of granite under a sledge hammer. Then they took a knife blade to his face, neck, throat, tongue, and the strings of vocal cords that strained with tension at the terror held before them. They left him for dead on his hotel room floor. Against all odds, Joe E. Lewis survived and thus entered into legend while still alive. Over time he redeveloped his ability to speak, and froggishly sing, two salient features of his standup act which flourished for decades after at the highest, richest, levels of success in the game. In the 1940's he was the King of Miami Beach. Its most popular, well respected, and highest paid comic. The same was true across America. He was mainstream, with an edge that kept him cool, even in a tux.

SOPHIE
TUCKER
with TED SHAPIRO
in a
Spectacular Revue
TWICE NITELY
Latin Quarter
PALM ISLAND MIAMI BEACH
JAN MURRAY

DINNERS FROM 3.25
Sophie
TUCKER
WITH TED SHAPIRO
AT THE PIANO
Added Attraction
JACKIE
MILES
AMERICA'S NEWEST COMEDIAN
BOBBY
BREEN
DIRECT FROM HOLLYWOOD
JACK
STANTON
HOLLYWOOD COVER GIRLS
JOE CANDULLO AND HIS ORCH.
NO COVER
NO MINIMUM
IN PATIO
NED SCHUYLER'S
BEACHCOMBER
DINNER • SUPPER • RES. CALL MARTINI 58-2501
1271 DADE BLVD., MIAMI BEACH

NEW PRICE POLICY
$5..
INCLUDES
FULL COURSE
• DINNER
• FREE COCKTAIL
• DANCING • BILLY VINE
• THE GREAT SOPH TUCKER SHOW
Sophie
TUCKER
WITH TED SHAPIRO
AT THE PIANO
BILLY VINE
CBS COMEDY & TELEVISION STAR
THE SZONYS
FRANK LINALE ORCHESTRA
BUSTER BURNELL
JUNE TAYLOR DANCERS
Ned Schuyler's
Beachcomber
1271 DADE BLVD • Phone 58-2501

SOPHIE TUCKER

Sophie Tucker did what a lot of women wanted to do in the early 1900's. She ditched her son and husband, ran off to New York City and became a self made showbiz millionaire. The funny misdirect about Sophie Tucker, "Last Of The Red Hot Mamas," is that she was a dirty little ghetto immigrant who made herself into a princess. Then a Queen. She wasn't exactly a standup comic, but she helped pioneer standup comedy. Her sixty years of live shows employed music, one liners, jokes, set ups, punchlines, gags, crowd work and the incongruous elegance of her soulful emotional appeals, with fat lady comedic presence. She would dress in elaborate and expensive gowns, hair done to the nines, dripping jewels. In 1946, Sophie Tucker was announced in the Miami Herald making $5,000 a week at the Latin Quarter. The Latin Quarter was a Florida branch of the famous New York nightclub founded by Lou Walters (the news lady Barbara Walter's father). This Walters guy had clubs all over the U.S. doing Parisian style revues of comedy, burlesque, music, and utilizing atmosphere to create memorable parties. Miami's Latin Quarter was on Palm Island, a manmade haven in the Biscayne Bay built from reclaimed fill from dynamiting suburban canals. It was located between Miami and Miami Beach, down by where all the Cruise Ships go through today, but on the north side of the causeway. It's next to Star Island and Hibiscus Island, full of mafia and pop culture history. Al Capone and lots of other gangsters kept houses there. Sophie Tucker was American royalty, but from a low down dirty mud hovel of a murderous gossiping shtetl in a frozen godforsaken Ukrainian tundra, who because of her efforts in performing into new technology, lives forever. In February of 1948, she was the Queen Of Hearts at a benefit for the Hellinger Heart Show, an "All-star studded event" featuring Milton Berle, Lucille Ball, Desi Arnaz, and The Vagabonds. The party took place at the Lord Tarleton Hotel at 41st and Collins Ave for a ten dollar donation, which wasn't chump change back then, so it must have been a pretty fancy crowd. She worked glamorous venues like the Beachcomber in 1947 with dinners from $3.25. That same year, she dropped a swinging jazzy blues version of "Some Of These Days" that will rock your soul if you've got one. Great band, arrangement, and vocal performance. Sophie Tucker used to collect everyone's house address and business information in a book she carried with her at all times, and she would send out physical invites to her shows through every city that she toured. She never used a secretary. She did everything herself. The original mailing list. Real high class dame in all expensive clothes and furs and jewelry, but she made the whole thing up. Born in a Ukrainian part of Imperial Russia with a target on her head and armies of blood-thirsty-Jew-killing maniacs trying to exterminate her family, her parents took her as a baby to America and opened a greasy deli selling pastrami on rye to longshoremen on the Connecticut river. The family worked there all hours. Little Sophie grew up in the kitchen, at the register, or dancing for pennies on the bar top. Rosy cheeked Ukrainian peasant, she grew stout against the Connecticut winters. Sophie had curves and her curves had curves. People called her fat and she heard it all the time. But she married young and had a son by 19, along with big dreams that went against popular convention. Tucker had the confidence of a headline star. So she left her baby with her sister, fired her husband, kept his name, and showed up on the cold shoulder of the snowed in streets of New York City and somehow found a singing job. She worked blackface, covered in the soot makeup of burnt cork to appease the racial humor of Vaudeville, until one day she kicked her show-trunk off the back of a train and went on stage with her blonde hair flying wild and the crowd went crazy. She started making more money and then one fateful day she bought the sheet music for a new song from a black songwriter named Shelton Brooks. It was called "Some Of These Days," and it became her signature hit for over sixty years. Every time a record sold or played on the radio, the credited writer, Shelton Brooks, got paid. Imagine that. Black songwriter getting rich off a Jew lady making his song a hit. Beautiful. "Some Of These Days" is one of the first platinum singles. Sophie cut it in 1911 for Edison Recordings, as in Thomas Edison, whose company invented audio stored on tubes, before records existed. By being so early, "Some Of These Days" was automatically historic, and the novelty of it meant everyone was talking about it. And every time a new medium came along, Sophie was one of the first on it. Records, radio, silent films, talkies, television. She developed a royal stage show where she wore $30,000 gowns, and performed double entendre and self deprecating music and comedy with her lifelong piano accompanist Ted Shapiro, and throughout the decades, she always ended up in Miami like all good aging European Jews chasing sunshine and good times, thirsty with a party dress, draped in fur and dripping pearls. Yet still described by NYC columnist O.O. McIntyre as a "coon shouter," for her rough and ready black sound. Sort of an early female Elvis. Comedy version. She always liked being around black people ever since working the deli on the docks of the Connecticut River. Sophie Tucker was in show business for over sixty years, going back to the earliest days of mass communication through recorded audio/visual media. By 1921, Trixie Thomas promoters spent over two years on ad buys in the Miami Herald billing her as the "Sophie Tucker Of The South." There were women all over the states calling themselves "The Sophie Tucker Of...." wherever they were from. The real Tucker was a highly photogenic and talented artist, but she played into the elephant in the room. A heavyweight with a pretty face; a voice like red velvet cake and a wit like an immigrant. A self-made, bootstrapped American mogul of the highest order in the greatest tradition of the country's high ideals. She was friends with seven presidents. She was in a running card game with Al Capone. She lent a dress to J Edgar Hoover from the FBI when he asked if she had a dress for him to wear. She would eat steaks with Frank Sinatra and Sammy Davis Jr. at their favorite stripclub on Biscayne Boulevard, because the road was her life but Miami's where she made a home, and there are decades of shows at all of the best venues to look back on and see her name and regal face. She was paid, she was made, and Ed Sullivan dedicated a whole one-hour special of his show to her for her birthday in 1963, live from the Fontainebleau Hotel in Miami Beach.

CONTINENTAL CLUB
6000 NW 7th Ave.
100% AIR CONDITIONED

Here Comes The Judge

"SOUL SHAKE"
"PICKING WILD MOUNTAIN BERRIES"

"HERE COMES THE JUDGE"

"THE HORSE"
"SWITCH IT ON"

Thursday MAY 15
ONE NITE ONLY!
3-Shows
5 P.M.
8:30 P.M.
11 P.M.

5 P.M. FAMILY SHOW
– NO ALCOHOL SOLD

"YOU SEEN MY WIFE"

"I KNOW I'VE GOT A SURE THING"

ADVANCE TICKETS NOW ON SALE:
PIGMEAT MARKHAM is coming to Miami in one of the biggest all-star shows of all times. See in person the world famous PIGMEAT MARKHAM plus PEGGY SCOTT and JO JO BENSON "Soul Shake", "Picking Wild Mountain Berries," CLIFF NOBLES & CO., "The Horse", "Switch It On". Also OLLIE AND THE NIGHTINGALES "I Know I've Got a Sure Thing." See all these great stars Thurs., May 15, One Night Only at the World Famous Continental Club, 6000 NW 7th Avenue. 3 Big Shows. Special Early Matinee showing 5 p.m. Admission $3.00. Bring the family. No alcohol sold. 2nd show: 8:30 p.m., adm. $4.50. 3rd Show: 11 p.m. until. adm. $5.50. Tickets now on sale at United Record Shop, 6265 NW 7th Avenue, Continental Cleaners, 798 NW 62nd Street, Susie's Wig & Beauty Salon, 7616 NW 22nd Ave., Tropical Record Co., 4950 NW 7th Ave., Patricia's Inc., 5843 NW 17th Ave., Jackson's Market, 5830 NW 12th Ave., Mr. Walters Wig Shop, 6011 NW 7th Avenue.

PIGMEAT MARKHAM

Pigmeat goes way back so far in comedy that he used to hold the two-month-old Sammy-baby Davis Jr. backstage while his Mom was on stage with the chorus. Sweet Poppa Pigmeat, real name Dewey Alamo Markham, started in comedy at the age of 14, when he ran off with a traveling carnival with some friends. His first job, he did skits and songs with his neighborhood pals for $1.50 a week. Back then teenagers used run off with a show to go make money all the time. Markham took to it. One year in, he joined The Florida Blossoms minstrel show. Pigmeat is so old that he was before, during, and after his time. Black guy so funny he had to wear black face just so people would think he was white, white people pretending to be black being the highest form of acceptable comedy at the time. At the time being way back when he started in 1918. Man had to wear blackface for the first twenty years of his comedy career. Even wore blackface at The Apollo. And he held the record for most Apollo performances for a long time. Crowd loved Pigmeat. Blackface at the Apollo. Those uptown Harlem renaissance cats could not stand it. Got so the black intelligentsia openly hated his comedy, criticized and ridiculed him. Tried to clown him, but he got the laughs. People loved

Pigmeat. His audiences were all black for almost his entire laugh. He could be brash, loud, rude, abrasive, but clever wordplay, expert timing, rapid fire back and forth banter with his on-stage comic foils essentially performing their era's short form content - skits, or "situations" as he called them - woven into the double helix of the art form in part thanks to him hitting the road independent for all of those decades before a video clip exploded his popularity. The American psyche. Fractured mess. A broken mirror pointed at a raging river, but Dewey Alamo was there. Still is. "Sock it to me!" "Here come the judge!" His big hit was, "Here Come The Judge!" and the big payoff of the gag was that he would slap people over the head with a cow bladder filled with water and it would make this great smacking sound that rang out if it was mic'd up or not. He had a friend get the cow bladders for him straight from the slaughterhouse. I believe this is the origin and inspiration for the Homie The Clown routine from Damon Wayans on the landmark 1990's television sketch comedy show In Living Color. Pigmeat Markham's show was based in what he called situations that consisted of repetition, rapid fire dialogue, get-it jokes, puns, wordplay, high volume, powerful delivery, and accelerated joke velocity. Back to back punches. Markham had a big face with a tectonic geography he could affect from a state of confident tranquility to a tempest of emotion through facial muscle movements that were visible from space, or at least the back of any room. This skill carried him from comedy's industrial revolution through its technological one, from touring with a minstrel show in a private train car, to selling a million vinyl records off a a big tv shoutout. Markham went hard on the road, had his wife on the road, his life on the road. Steel horse full of wild comedians pulling up to one little coal mine or tobacco town after another. Having a ball. Bring out his big old boss hog bass drum and march the goof troop right through the middle of the street to the center of town to go drum up business for the show. That's how they used to do it. Street barking, carnival style. They had that big old tent that would hold over a thousand people, laughing joy into its canvas in each and every town. Hecklers like you've never seen or heard. Beautiful chorus girls. Kids sneaking under the flapjacks of the tabernacle to hilarity kicking up dust. Snack oil bubbling in the heat. Mystery drinks in various flavors. One act after another building the crowd into a roiling super-consciousness. A laugh-powered hive-mind finely tuned to each and every movement and energy, truth and lie, intention, denial, fact, facsimile, and facetious statement held by the ankles of comedy over the purifying absolution of audience approval.

That was the show, night after night of its various trudgeries and drudgeries across the landscape of America for forty years, fortunes coming and going like a woman in the night, until one fine Hallelujah, when Little Sammy Davis Jr. was all grown up now, and he riffed on that old Markham classic "Here come da judge!" on a national TV show called Laugh-In, which was young and hip, and somehow counterculture and mainstream at the same time; thus bringing new life to the road-tested, time-proven Pigmeat trademark sloganeering. The man was back. Pig. Dewey Alamo. Sweet Poppa Pigmeat. He always made a pretty good living. But a thousand bucks a week went to five, then seven, then ten thousand bucks a week, and kept on climbing. He got his time, he got his money, he made his mark, he helped the next generation. Originator. Funny man. Comedian. Stand up guy.

After fifty years in the business, he found himself on stage at the Continental Club at 6000 NW 7th Ave, Liberty City, formerly the King Of Hearts. Nice place. 100% air conditioned. One night only. Three big shows. Five p.m. family show, no alcohol sold, then an eight o'clock and an eleven o'clock show. He brought his friends with him. Peggy Scott, Jo Jo Benson, Cliff Nobles, Ollie And The Nightingales. Advance tickets were available all over Liberty City, at United Record Shop,

Tropical Record Co., Susie's Wig and Beauty Salon, Jackson's Market, Mr. Walters Wig Shop, Susie's Wig and Beauty Salon. There'd be classic skits like, "The Horse," "Picking Wild Mountain Berries," "Soul Shake," and "Switch It On." The poster in the Miami Times newspaper said Here Comes The Judge and tickets cost $3. That's a popular rate. Pigmeat's Markham's book, called Here Come The Judge! hit the stores in 1969. It's one of the best comedy books out there.

Direct From

THE SMOTHERS BROTHERS
and
MERV GRIFFIN SHOWS

JACKIE
"MOMS"

MABLEY

Direct From
JOEY BISHOP SHOW

JACKIE
"HIGHER
and
HIGHER"

WILSON

BIM-BAM-BOO TRIO
"New Soul Sound"

BILLY STEWART & BAND
"Summertime"

EXTRA ADDED!
DIANE & THE RAVENETTES
"Baby Pull My Heartstrings"

"SOUL REVIVAL"

MIAMI STADIUM

SAT. JAN. 20th at 8:30 P.M.

TICKETS NOW ON SALE at Miami Stadium box office; Economy Drug, NW 7th Ave. & NW 3rd Ave.; Community Drug, NW 15th Ave.; Band Box Barber Shop, NW 2nd Ave.; United Radio & TV, NW 7th Ave.; Mr. Big, NW 2nd Ave.; Spec's, S. Dixie Hwy.; Sunshine Tours, Northside Shopping Ctr.; Record Bar, Miracle Mile, Gables; Miami Beach Radio Co., Lincoln Rd.; Melody Music, Hollywood; and Spin City Record Store, Ft. Lauderdale.

ADVANCE GEN. ADMISSION $2
(AT GATE $2.50) RES. $3.50 • $4.50

MOMS MABLEY

It's sad to say how tragedy begets comedy, but Moms Mabley had already been raped, robbed, beaten, had her kids stolen, and her parents killed in bad circumstances before she was even eighteen years old. She'd already been in showbiz four years, after she ran off from her little home town of Brevard, North Carolina in 1911 and joined a traveling minstrel show, where she faced more of the criminal hardships she was already accustomed to: with sexual abuse, forced labor, and bad conditions some of the pre-requisites to her trailblazing life in entertainment. By the end of her career, she was filling stadiums as a standup comic. Solo act. Headliner. Her many albums, some of the most popular of which were major label conceptual dialogues between herself and political figures, sold millions. She'd been a star of stage and screen, written a book, exploded with television popularity late in life, and effectively raised herself into the protective matriarchal character she played on stage, whom she created as a defense mechanism against the cruelties around every corner in a typical lifetime. But even at the end, in the midst of all that fame and acclaim, arena headline money, power, and respect, good old Moms Mabley was only one degree of separation from organized crime, targeted high value robberies, jewel theft, wire fraud, interstate racketeering, luxury bandits, identity theft, and kidnapping. And it all centers on two concert promoters and a big show in Miami.

Miami Herald
July 24, 1969

Stage Shows a Front for Theft Act?
By James Savage

"A pair of Miami's better known felons have got into show business.

In April, John Clarence Cook and Sam Urbana tried to book Miami Stadium for a one night stand to stage a Negro rock review headlined by comedienne Moms Mabley.

Miami Police rejected their stadium application."

That was in 1969, but in January 1968, an ad for Jackie Wilson and Moms Mabley at Miami Stadium appeared in the Miami Herald, and a writeup in the same edition explained that this would be the first in a series of soul festivals. Motor City soul powerhouse Jackie Wilson had just hit with "Higher & Higher" and Moms was celebrating 44 years in showbiz. There is no review I can find saying how it went. There's also no way to know if the same promoters were throwing the followup show at the same place, with the same lineup, one year later, but the salient details suggests yes. When the Miami Police denied the permit for the 1969 event, the tag team of theatrical promoters known as Forte Productions, Sam Urbana and John Clarence Cook, took the show and headed off to Tampa, Florida; Shreveport, Louisiana; and Fort Worth, Texas, and ads in those cities' newspapers confirm those promotions.

Here's the deal. Sam Urbana was a lower level mobster and a good soldier with bad timing who had two burglary convictions up north; and he was highly connected to the Chicago Mafia, to Paul "The Waiter" Ricca, to Anthony "Big Tuna" Accardo, and to Sam "Big Moe" Giancana. Those were major businessmen. Urbana also ran with Gerald "Ding Dong" Carusiello and Peter Bartemio, jewel thieves who caught seventy five year bids for their craft.

Urbana heisted jewelry, flew stolen checks, committed fraud, and had 22 arrests on his record when he showed up to Miami with no visible source of income, hanging with shady characters, and operating out of an apartment at 454 NE 23rd street that the FBI bugged as soon as he walked in the door in 1965. Urbana got busted for bank-checks that had been stolen in Detroit, got convicted, then freed on a bond order by Judge Joe Eaton after his lawyer Frank Ragano appealed his no-bond order in a case that went to the Supreme Court for the rights of mobsters to keep doing business on the outside while fighting their convictions on appeal. A crucial ruling actually. And, watch how this all comes together, his conviction got overturned because he wasn't allowed to examine the transcripts of the secret wiretaps the FBI was running on him that the cops exposed by kicking down his door. That was June 29th, 1969.

The government said they were such bad guys, but how bad could they be if Moms Mabley was their favorite comedian.

When Urbana first showed up to the city, the Miami Herald wrote a series of investigative pieces on corruption and the criminal underworld. Urbana became a target for the local cops and the feds as well. A grand jury got involved. Every move he made, they were watching him. Couldn't even take a shit without them saying who farted. They were watching him drink with his cronie William Berg at the 500 Klub on 36th street and 27th

Ave., according to Jon Nordheimer in a Miami Herald front page story. Captain Roy Longbottom and Lieutenant Charles Black from the sheriff's office said hello. Urbana became agitated, raised his voice, the cops arrested him for profanity, with an added charge of vagrancy, "Because he couldn't show visible means of support." The cops had the nerve to tell the bar manager that Urbana was an undesirable element and shouldn't be served or even allowed entry. Ironically, the wife of Berg, the guy that Urbana was drinking with, was the head of the corporation that had just purchased the liquor license to the place.

Urbana was under heavy surveillance and out on bond, hanging with a character named John Clarence Cook, a sophisticated high stakes jewel thief who had been arrested and gone to trial over and over again but never been convicted.

Cops did a kick-door on a pad Urbana was staying at and found cash, conflicting reports between $6,000 - $8,000, a .25 automatic pistol, and some weed, but the case ended up getting thrown out for illegal search. He was in there with a prostitute and his pal, another jewel thief.

After their permit got denied for the 1969 edition of Moms Mabley at Miami Stadium, while on tour, Sam Urbana and John Clarence Cook got arrested for pulling a gem heist at a country club north of San Diego. According to authorities, the guys were using the Moms Mabley and Jackie Wilson shows as a cover to pull elaborate robberies, breaking into targeted guest rooms at luxury hotels.

After posting bond, Federal Judge Joe Eaton allowed the guys to continue operating their theatrical booking agency as long as they "notified federal officials of what states they're traveling to," and agreeing to send regular wired communications on their whereabouts to Miami police.

So while Moms was on stage, putting butts in the seats, her promoters were doing B&E's, robbing gems on the creep. Some questions occur. Was she getting paid properly and in a timely manner for her shows? What did she know? How did she get involved? Was she secretly in the mafia? Did she call the hit on Jimmy Hoffa? I think some of the answers are covered in her many comedy albums, such as Live at Sing Sing Prison from 1970, or perhaps, I Got Somethin To Tell You from 1963.

One thing is for certain, Moms dropped a serious record called "Abraham, Martin, and John," written by Dick Holler about Abraham Lincoln, Martin Luther King Jr., John Lennon, and Bobby Kennedy that will bring a tear to your eye.

Tear to your eye is all that Urbana and John Clarence Cook seemed to have. In July 1970, Urbana got arrested on the ninth hole of a Miami-Dade golf course. He was accused of holding $25,000 worth of dirty gold that'd been hijacked between Italy and the MIA. In April of 1971, John Clarence Cook got convicted by a jury for doing criminal-arbitrage on five million stolen U.S. Postal Stamps worth an estimated $395,000 on the black market. He bought them from a thief for 70% face value, and then sold them to crooked postal workers in NYC for 80% face value. He got 12 years federal prison for it.

In 1975, Urbana was robbed at gunpoint outside his business for his cash, watch, rings, chains, and car and he had to call the cops. In 1989, he got busted for running a mobbed up pawn shop, exotic car importer, and for pulling more high end heists, loansharking, insurance fraud, bookmaking, and laundering a million bucks in dirty cash through a bingo parlor in Maryland. He pled guilty.

This is the shit Moms Mabley had to deal with all the way up to the end of her career cause she was born in 1894 and died in 1975. Pretty much from reconstruction to the mafia. But then again, maybe Sam Urbana and John Clarence Cook were her favorite promoters and maybe they always loved her and treated her right, just like Moms Mabley always deserved.

MARCO POLO
HYATT HOUSE

OPENING TUESDAY
JANUARY 28
"THE ANGRY YOUNG COMEDIAN"

RODNEY DANGERFIELD

in Indies Show Lounge
JERRY MARSHALL ORCHESTRA
2 Shows Nitely 10 & 12
3 Shows Wk. Ends 9:30-11-12:30
Also in the INDIES SHOW LOUNGE
JOE VENTO of "THE 3 SUNS"
At the Wurlitzer Organ
From 5:00 P.M. to 8:00 P.M.

OPEN HEARTH STEAKS

in the Sultan's Table
COMPLETE CHAR-BROILED DINNERS
AL MARTIN — AT THE PIANO
7:00 P.M. to 10:00 P.M.

MARCO POLO HYATT HOUSE
On The Ocean • 192nd & Collins, Miami Beach
FREE PARKING • For Reservations, Call 949-1461

RODNEY DANGERFIELD

Jacob Cohen was a joke-hustling teenage comic working New York City and The Borscht Belt as a singing waiter named Jack Roy, son of comic juggler Phil Roy, who used to be Phil Cohen before he got into Vaudeville. Jack got disillusioned working two-bit shuffles in the Catskils for fat-face latke-pigs that couldn't hear him and didn't care what he had to say, and were too busy eating pork chops on garlic toast either way. It wasn't kosher. He drove a laundry truck two days a week, a fish truck the two other, pursued standup two nights a week, and had one day off. At night he wrote jokes. The harder he worked, the less work he had. It didn't make cents. George Washington sat in his pocket alone and died of boredom. Nothing was doing. So he got married and went into the aluminum siding and watching-paint-dry business off the tower of Babylon, Long Island somewhere and tried to forget all about comedy.

But the paint fumes slowly drove him crazy. Even crazier than he was already. That's when his wife, the miserable cunt (just kidding), left him. He'd been trying to sell jokes to younger talent, but there wasn't any. So he had to do it himself. He went twenty grand in debt at the age of 42 and worked his way back into the funny business the hard way. Working clubs for nothin' and nobody. He was in the red like a Jew at an Irish whorehouse. One day, a New York club owner named George McFadden gave him the name Rodney Dangerfield and that's when his life started.

Today, he's still everyone's favorite comic. Whether they like him or not. Rodney Dangerfield is America. He's dirty. Clean. Funny. Mean. He's angry. Nice. A smoker, a drinker, a .. a recreational coke sniffer, an animal. A husband, a father, a showman, a professional. A funny face with a dark heart. Or is it a gloomy face with a funny soul? A loser and a millionaire. A handsome, confident mug, and an ugly bug eyed sex freak. He's a smoker, and a breath of fresh air. Rodney Dangerfield: The most respected least respected man in show business. Dead since 2004, and still the funniest guy alive. Dangerfield will never die.

Where's his narrative feature, documentary movie, 42 hour episodic series? Think of it now. Leonardo DiCaprio as Rodney Dangerfield.

Things don't always go how they're supposed to. His legendary club in New York City, where Seinfeld killed relentlessly and Andrew

Dice Clay recorded his classic double album with Rick Rubin, The Day The Laughter Died, went outta business (someone just bought the place). His name and likeness have been licensed to a novelty toilet paper company called Life Stinks started by Mel Brook's third cousin twice removed (just kidding). He's gone, but he's a moneymaker, and the Chinese global asset management company that owns his IP still lets us see a few of his movies every year (just kidding). What's the one with the golf club and the bucktooth rat, with Chevy Chase & Bill Murray…Caddyshack. It was filmed at the Rolling Hills Country Club in Davie, Florida ten miles west of the beach, just north of Hollywood, just south of Fort Lauderdale, and every day on set was a cocaine-golf-cart liquor-fueled reefer-mad pilled-out sexed-up lawn party that lasted eleven weeks and through a category 2 hurricane in 1979. Every night in the clubs, on the streets, and in the hotel suites was a party.

Rodney liked South Florida. His sister and nephew lived in Broward County. He was a regular visitor. His father loved Miami Beach and retired to it in the land of surf, sun, and pastrami on rye, dying in the MIA in 1971. RIP. He's buried west of the city at Lakeside Memorial in Doral. A funny Russian Jew. He was born in 1893 for fucks sake. When he started comedy, Shakespeare was still stealing jokes.

You know who stole jokes from Rodney? Everybody. Especially Milton Berle. That cocksucka sonofabitch would walk right into Rodney's show in Vegas with a tape recorder and steal jokes. Used to piss Rodney off bad, he said it right in the newspaper.

In January 1969, Rodney Dangerfield was the headliner at the Marco Polo Hyatt House, billed as the "Angry Young Comedian," live with open hearth steaks at the Sultan's Table, with complete char-broiled dinners on the ocean at 192nd and Collins.

In reference to this show, Miami News writer Herb Kelly, who spent time talking to comics in the clubs and in the streets, reported that "Comedian Rodney Dangerfield, now playing the Marco Polo Hyatt House, is spending a lot of time with his dad, Phil Roy, 76, who lives in Miami Beach. Roy was in Vaudeville, half of the team of Roy Arthur."

The Arthur was Rodney's uncle, real name Adolf. Philip and Adolf Cohen legally changed their names to Phil Roy and Roy Arthur and had a tag-team comedy act that did juggling, and wacky slapstick.

I found a yellowed old description of their show on a find-a-grave website with a listing, description, and photos added by a user named Census Taker. The text of the yellowed show description reads, in part, "Phil Roy is an exceedingly dexterous juggler, and does an astounding number of adroit feats. His associate, Roy Arthur, for comedy purposes, is as awkward as Phil Roy is nimble." According to a listing for Rodney's Uncle Adolf located on the same findagrave.com website, once again added by the user Census Taker (member profile 46879037), Uncle Adolf's nickname was "Bunky," and he was the oldest of the family born to Jacob and Sarah (Adelson) Cohen. Rodney was named after his grandfather. Uncle Bunky got started in comedy early. He was born in Philly in 1887 and died in LA in 1953. He did blackface. He played a buffoon to a famous juggler named Jean Bedini. He got his friend Eddie Cantor a gig on the circuit, and the kid blew up to be a big Hollywood star. On his way up, working through the theaters of NYC, little Rodney Dangerfield got to sit front row at Eddie's shows, but he wasn't laughing at Cantor's jokes, so they put him all the way in the back. Then he started laughing like crazy, overreacting, and when they asked him what the deal was, little Rodney Dangerfield said he was trying to work his way back up to the front.

One of the Vaudeville show routines that Rodney's dad and Uncle Bunky did was called, "Chinese Restaurant." Phil would juggle all these crazy plates and his brother would drop them in a funny way, sort of like in the Rodney Dangerfield movie Easy Money with Joe Pesci. Wedding cake scene.

So there you have it. Rodney Dangerfield was born to be funny.

What he used to like most about Miami was sitting around on the balcony of whatever condo on the beach he was staying at, spark up a fat ass joint, and sit there in his robe and slippers getting high as fuck with his dick and balls out getting fresh air in the sunshine and the ocean breeze while giving himself the respect he deserved. Probably jacking off.

Motherfucker was a millionaire with a Grammy Award for his 1980 comedy album No Respect, on Casablanca Records, the same label as KISS. Freaky young women were all over him. The older he got, his audience stayed college age. In 1982 he had a big show at the Sunrise Musical Theater by special request of John Lomelo, the guy who discovered Sam & Dave and helped start Flip Wilson. The guy who got a $30,000 Rolex watch given to him on stage by Frank Sinatra when he booked him, as Mayor, to open Sunrise Musical Theater (paying him a couple hundred thousand out of the city budget or close to it).

The Miami Herald ran the First And Last Rodney Dangerfield Look-Alike and Monologue Contest on the front page of the Living Today section. It asked for people to, "Send us a mugshot of your miserable mug," or 'send ten no-respect jokes,' for a chance to win two free tickets to the show. On April 22nd, 1982, they said, "No More Calls, We Have Our Losers!"

But let's go back a few years before that, to 1978, when Rodney Dangerfield was one of the stars of the most successful ad campaign in television history at the time, the marketing of Miller Lite beer, which began in 1975 through a series of tv commercials featuring hyper masculine ex-athletes, like Joe Frazier, Dick Butkus, and John Madden, plus Rodney Dangerfield, drinking lite beer, which was considered "sissy" up till then. Rodney was in at least six of the so-called "Great Taste, Less Filling" commercials, with aliens, on the golf course, at the bar, and with sexy ladies, as part the campaign extolling the virtues of this wondrous grog of an elixir for the everyday working man.

One of those commercials was shot on Key Biscayne in 1978, and featured the manly hardboiled noir and crime-fiction writer Mickey Spillane, plus Rodney Dangerfield, along with an all star sports cast of Nick Buoniconti, Billy Martin, Whitey Ford, Ray Nitschke, Matt Snell, Marv Throneberry, Ben Davidson, Tommy Heinsohn, Bubba Smith, Deacon Jones, Paul Hornung, Bernard "Boom Boom" Geoffrion, Mendy Rudolph, Phil Rizzuto, Billy Martin, and "Grits" Gresham. The day before shooting, the cast were wined and dined at the ritzy Palm-Aire Club in Pompano, at a cocktail party to announce the beer commercial. Cocktail party to announce a beer commercial? Yea, it was all cocks in the room and no tail. Just a lot of lite beer.

The commercial was shot on April Fool's Day at Crandon Park Beach, on the historic barrier island four miles south of South Beach, five and a half miles east of mainland Miami, and fifty three miles west of North Bimini, Bahamas. Beautiful shooting location over the years for everything from furniture commercials to internet porn videos.

The concept of the ad was that half the guys were pulling one side of a rope in a tug of war between "Tastes Great," and the other side were pulling for "Less Filling!" These were the two big selling points of Miller Lite and the epic battle of the athletes centered on their impossible-to-decide bout, which climaxed when two hot swimsuit chicks walked by and led everyone off to a Miller Lite party on the beach.

There's a Miami Herald article about it, by a dork named Barry. Had the damn nerve to say about Rodney, "He looked like a bean bag chair perched on two twigs." So I looked up the writer and he looks like he just shit-his-pants. In every picture! What a loser. Like a Silly Putty peanut came to life and fell face first on a dirty barber shop floor. And got stepped on.

Jacob Cohen created Rodney Dangerfield as an avatar for people to project their own insecurities on. A character. A comic voice. A perspective with a big contingent in the population of the collective unconscious. A symbol for the underdog in all of us. Fighting through a world of haters to get on Johnny Carson 65 times. Dangerfield got plenty of respect. People only slick their hair back when they like how they look. In the commercial he looks tan and healthy.

Another one of the places Rodney Dangerfield was seen in Miami was with The Supremes, minus Diana Ross, in April 1966 in the Casanova Room at the Deauville Hotel at 67th and Collins.

In 1969, in an article by Frank Langley outta New York, that ran in the Fort Lauderdale News, Rodney Dangerfield talked about opening his own club, which he did. But he had plans to expand. He said, "I'm even thinking of opening a second one in Miami that's called Dangerfield South. People tell me I'm nuts. They say I can't do it…They all tried and failed. Do I take the advice of failures? I think I can do it. I know I can….My father always said behind every lucky guy you'll find a brain."

Dangerfield's South never happened, but in 1977, Rodney was booked to play the Colonial Inn Motel, oceanfront at 181st and Collins Ave in Sunny Isles Beach for $8.50 per person, which included two drinks. Jack Ross was the MC. There was free parking. And there was a live orchestra and dancing. It was a nice place with a nine hole professional putting green, nightly dancing and entertainment, 3 pools, a 500' foot beach, complete breakfast, gourmet dinners, and all the amenities of a complete resort motel. Rodney Dangerfield always did like a good motel party. And he respected an all you can eat buffet.

KING OF HEARTS CLUB

FRI - SAT - SUN JULY 29-30-31

Big FLOOR SHOW

"The UNTOUCHABLE"

PHIL HARRIS

Your Master of Ceremonies

Sam Moore & Dave Prater

MIAMI'S NEWEST SINGING SENSATIONS

SAM MOORE AND DAVE PRATER

Willie Lee Mack
Sultry Singing Sensation

Eloise Forman
Popular Recording Star

Vanilla Williams
Shake Dancer Supreme

Music by
W. C. Baker's Band

Featuring
Clara Jay
Terrific Blues Singer

Big Special Show
Beginning Thursday, August 4, once a month, produced and directed by "The Untouchable" Phil Harris.

For Reservations Call PL 8-2339 - Jack Corbitt **Admission 50c**

"The Untouchable" Phil Harris presents every Wednesday night his . . .

Original Big Amateur and Professional Hour
3 CASH PRIZES

J. G. PERLMUTTER ENTERPRISES
Presents the

SAM and DAVE

BIG SHOW

Sunday, Jan. 8th

WITH 10-PIECE ORCHESTRA
Featuring Kim Tolliver

Dinner Key Auditorium

DOORS OPEN 6 P.M.

HEAR SAM & DAVE SING "YOU AIN'T NO BIG THING," "YOU GOT ME HUMMING" "HOLD ON I 'M COMING,"

Student Tickets $2.50 Advance 3.00 At Door 3.50

WILDMAN STEVE OF WMBM, M.C.

J.G. PEARLMUTTER **SUN., JAN. 8**

Presents in Person at Dinner Key Auditorium

SAM & DAVE

DOUBLE DYNAMITE

"Hold On, I'm Coming"
"You Got Me Humming"

Plus

KIM TOLLIVER
THE CHAR-MELS
"Knock On Wood Man"
JIM TATUM
CHUCK A LUCK
And

The

SAM & DAVE

BIG 10-PC. ORCHESTRA

WMBM M.C. WILDMAN STEVE

Tickets Now on Sale at Box Office

DOORS OPEN 7 P.M.

Lomelo's...

King O' Hearts Club

THE NEWEST AND MOST BEAUTIFUL IN MIAMI

6000 N.W. 7th AVENUE

Welcoming FAMU and Langston Fans

PRESENTS

SPECIAL CLASSIC FLOOR SHOW

Sammy Moore

AND

Dave Prater

Miami 1960 Singing Sensations

E. LOIS FOREMAN

The Year's Greatest Singing Discovery

Phil *"Untouchable"* Harris

The One and Only Master of Ceremony

FLIP WILSON

"The Master of Comedy"

CLARA JAY—Queen of the Blues

W. C. BAKER'S BAND—Featuring Happy Rose, the man with the Horn

WELCOME OPEN HOUSE

MATINEE SATURDAY, DEC. 10

Fish Ray, The Sand Man, and his Calypsonians

SAM MOORE

Sam Moore is a Miami Pioneer, a Rock And Roll Hall Of Famer, a Grammy Lifetime Achievement Award Winner, and a pop vocal powerhouse and make-you-cry crooner as important to the history of pop, rock, country, soul, funk, and R&B as James Brown, Sam Cooke, Otis Redding, and Aretha Franklin, all friends of his from a life in music that he is still here as the Champion of today. I got the opportunity to interview him in 2015 for a book of collected interviews that I published called A People's History of Overtown Vol. 1 and I'm reprinting that interview here so that you can read about the true history of the real Miami.

2015 Interview (Questions redacted for narrative flow)

"I was thinking today, and talking after all the years, I would say 60 years that I been in the business...I been around the corner more than once and I was thinking some things, talking to my daughter, and I don't know. I never understood why you always hear about Motown and this and that and you go, wait a minute...you see these guys all on the TV, but what about Sam and Dave? Really!!!??! It didn't start bothering me until my 60s. I say, "Why Sam and Dave never got the notoriety that I really do believe we should have got?" I've thought about it and I can't tell you why. I never understood. I don't know why. Well, I guess let's start from the top.... I was actually born in Georgia. And then my mother and my grandmother and the rest of the family, my aunt, my cousins, and everybody migrated to Florida. My mother went to college in Georgia and she was a teacher there. I don't know what caused them to come to Florida. I was a baby. I was born in 1935. All I ever knew was Miami. I can't even tell ya about Georgia, other than maybe my grandma saying she was going to go visit her mother. I think once or twice she may have taken me on a train to Georgia. I was a little boy. But I was raised in Miami. The first thing I recall is growing up Overtown. But I remember someone told me not long ago that it was first called Colored Town. I said, "Really? Never heard of it." I remember good times. To me things weren't bad. I just thought that's the way life presented itself. I went to Booker T Washington High School in Overtown, Miami, Florida. When I was a little boy my grandmother worked for the family of the Kauffman's, a Jewish family on the beach and she did the washing and ironing and my mother actually did some of the bookkeeping and things of that nature. I was staying at 1455 NW 3rd Ave. I pushed my mind to remember that. Today it's gone. That was in the center of Overtown. Third Avenue, you could go across the street, down the corner, catch the bus and go downtown to go shopping and whatnot. I was around the Chinese and the Jews, and the blacks, the people of color. I don't go for all that African-American stuff. I was raised up around all that and I don't remember once being called the N word. I'm pretty sure I was, but I don't recall it. Everybody knew each other. Our rent wasn't what it would be today. Across the street was a shoe shop where you could get your shoes fixed, a grocery market, a pawn shop, a Ma and Pa place. Upstairs of the shoe place was a rooming house and up and down, everything was right there. On the weekends sometimes we'd see the Wright Family. And from there came along Brother and Sister Pew.…they were man and wife but everybody called them Brother and Sister Pew. And sometimes we'd see Rosetta Tharpe come to town, and Marion Williams before she got with the Ward singers. We're really going back some. We would walk out the door and my auntie and her two girls lived upstairs over a bar. I was always getting in trouble. I would stay in my grandmother's room and look out the window, and she would say, "What are you doing there?!? Get out of there." I'd see the guys out back shooting dice, and guys getting girls up against the wall, and my grandma would ask me what I'm doing, and I'd say, "Oh grandma

I'm just sleeping." And she'd say, "No you're not!" It was all kinds of stuff. I learned a lot of stuff like that. And I was always getting in trouble for eyeballing. But one thing I didn't know is that we were poor. I never missed a meal. We were always home for dinner and make sure at night you're straight into your home, not in the street. I was home with grandma and my mother and most of the time be sitting out on the front porch. One time we were sitting there and a friend of ours named Sally was with us. She was on the front porch with us and sadly she didn't wanna go across the street cause her husband had been abusing and stalking her. The word stalking hadn't been used like that before. But I remember so vividly being a little boy and Sally said, "I guess I should go on home. I sure don't want to, but I hope he don't bother me." She was of course talking about her husband. Then she went across the street, went upstairs and we heard a big, "Pop! Pop! Pop!" And her husband killed her. He killed Sally. I didn't really understand what happened or take it serious, but I knew it happened. Then there were these guys that killed a policeman, and one of them escaped the jailhouse. They were the first blacks I knew that was going to get the death penalty. Their names were Wassie Blue, Limpy, and Fatback. Limpy is the one who escaped from the 19th floor of Dade County Jail. And my mother was so scared she was telling everybody to look out, look out for Limpy. That was a big deal. They caught him before the trial started and he got sentenced to death alongside Wassie Blue. As the years went on I got with a group as a background singer. Tony Bell put the group together. He robbed a Chinese place, and that was a big deal too. Then I got with John Macarthur, and he had a group that I sang tenor with as background in that group. On Sundays, I did gospel. I moved around a lot in the gospel field and built a reputation. On a good night you made $100 and on a bad night you may come out with $25, and you gotta share that with the other guys in the group. It wasn't enough, but....I was supposed to graduate high school in 1954 but I got caught up in the wrong place at the wrong time and got shot in my thigh, and it went through my leg. I still have a bullet in my calf. I got caught with a friend of mine's wife and I didn't know he was coming home. I was trying to run away and go out the window. My grandmother and mother turned their head and asked me what happened. I lied and said I went to work and was bringing home a check and got robbed. I was really up in the room with this woman and she start screaming, "Oh that sound like my husband!" I was so small she practically picked me up and threw me out the window. Her husband shot and it went through the glass and into my leg. I told my mother I was robbed. I told my grandmother I was robbed. Then they start asking me questions and sent me off to Jackson Memorial Hospital to get treated. When I got home they started asking me questions and eventually they caught me in my lies and that was that. "Oh you got robbed? Who robbed you? What valuables did they want? They beat you up? Why'd they shoot you if they got what they wanted?" They caught me and said, "Oh, you lying!" So I got in trouble and had to stay home for a long time. They said, "Look, these women gonna be the death of you." So then I had to go to Summer School. Infection set in in my leg and that's why it is how it is today. Then the next thing I knew, John put together a group and I was touring with the circus. It wasn't the Silas Green show. I used to love to go to the Silas Green show and sneak under the tent when they would bring their show to town when I was a little boy. No, I joined the World of Mirth out of Orlando, with an all-black cast just like Silas Green. The next thing I knew we went on the road and did our little touring. I wasn't out there that long but I was out there. And that was fun, that was nice. I was out on the road with the circus in like 1955, '56, or '57. It was so long ago it's hard to remember the exact dates.

When I got back I went into the gospel stuff. A dear friend of mine named Cleveland Johnson taught me how to put words together and write songs. He was a wannabe boxer who introduced me to Miami Beach. He used to train and fight out there, just over the bridge from Overtown. He was a fighter, but his passion was to sit down and write songs. Wonderful young man. Friend of mine. He taught me all this stuff and from there I started writing with another young man by the name of Clarence Reid. He went to school with us. Different class. But anyway we would sit there and write songs. I would come up with my own words. I knew how to place the words. I didn't know how to rhyme. Clarence and I were friends for years. He didn't really have that many friends on that side of town. It was wonderful to be around him. Next thing I knew he had a group called the Delmyras with Paul Kelly and those people. Next thing you know Clarence started writing over there and we didn't see each other no more. I had Paul on a show with me when he had a hot record, but I didn't see Clarence. I also remember Willie Armbrister. His sister Leotha Kenny was in a group with me. Willie got himself killed over by the movie house down the street from 15th street and NW 3rd Avenue. I was home at the time and heard about it and when I went to go look he was lying on the ground in a pool of blood by Goodbread Alley and the Bucket of Blood. Meanwhile, I got started singing with Dave Prater and he and I built up an audience for our act. We were even doing shows in Nassau, Bahamas and Cuba. Yeah. We was there. Bimini and all. We weren't no big stars, but the boys were over there, the you know who, and our manager Johnny Lomelo knew them and they would send us over to go do our 10, 15, 20 minutes. We were performing everybody else's material and nobody really listening. We'd get paid like $50 or $75 a piece, come back and open for the Sunday night show. We went to Cuba and Nassau with the Munnings. The Munnings were the family who owned the biggest club in all Bahamas. To the Munnings, Sam and Dave was no big deal. They had the big club, the big band, the big Bahamian stars. The one they loved was Little Willie John. He was big. We was still doing other people's material and they didn't define us as future stars. We used to go play Nassau, walk up and down the beach, barely any time for girls even. We had to get back to Miami in time for Dave to go to work as a short order cook in Overtown. Nobody ever thought we would be no bigger than what we were. We had a big audience at the King of Hearts, and locally we opened for a lot of big stars. We were the two black nobodies in music that played the Fontainebleau. We would go on stage by walking through the back, through the kitchen, and when we were done, right back through the kitchen and get the hell out of there. It was no big thing, but that's how a lot of those big entertainers got to know us cause we were there playing the opening for the main star. And they would always say, "Give Sam and Dave a hand!!!" So we got to be well known for daytime shows, and seemed like every Friday we were playing another Bar Mitzvah. We did so many of those. We got paid $25 a piece and all the food we could eat. We had a wonderful time doing those even though they were never able to teach us how to sing in Hebrew. They always tried though, and everybody would sing a Jewish song. The way I got started singing professionally in the first place was the King of Hearts Club in Liberty City. I caught myself trying to impress my buddies and friends coming by this club. It used to be a country and western place at first. You'd see people woohaw and all that and I never paid attention until one time I'm walking past, and I think Clarence Reid was amongst us, and I was the littlest guy in the group, so they dared me to sign up for the open mic or try to be an MC for the show. They know if they give me a dare, I'm gonna take it. They say, "I bet you won't go get that job…." So I went and told the owner, "I know how to be an MC, and sing, and tell jokes." And they said, "Where you worked at?" and I said, "The Fontainebleau." That was my first lie. He said, "You're an MC?" I said, "Yes, yes, yes. Yes!" But up until then I was just a little gospel singer, singing in church and lying to my mother. My mother didn't know I was over there. I was goin' to the King Of Hearts and telling her I was going to rehearsal for gospel. I would come home so tired. I didn't know I was poor. I had no inkling I would become this international pop, soul, rock, and R&B icon. I would stay out all night and come home to grandma. I had heard many records by the Dominoes and Clyde McPhatter and I liked the stuff they were doing. The first time I heard "60 Minutes Man," I didn't address that as Jackie Wilson. I just liked the song. Then I heard "Danny Boy," and wow, it was building up to my working on the beach and on the black part of Miami at the Sir John Knight Beat. And I didn't even know that Jackie Wilson and Sam Cooke knew each other. I got to be friends with Sam Cooke before I got to be friends with Jackie Wilson. When I first saw Jack in person I was preparing to go to Chicago to go out on the road with the Soul Stirrers. Sam had left the group and they needed a replacement for him. I guess he liked me enough to recommend me for the job. My voice wasn't as cultivated, but he still told the Soul Stirrers about me. I went and rehearsed with them and they liked my style, so they asked me to join the group as the lead singer. And I accepted. Right around that time I went over to the Knight Beat and saw Johnny Taylor and Jackie Wilson perform. I saw the name Jackie Wilson, Mr. Excitement and decided to check out the show, and what I saw changed the whole thing to what I became. The women, the girls, the boys, was all screaming at this man. And I thought, "That's what I wanna do!" I liked his cut, what he did on stage, his moves, spinning around, hair all falling in his face. I didn't know how to tell the Soul Stirrers about my change of heart. Show you how stupid I was. They were ready to take me that Sunday night. I ducked. They were going up to Chicago and I was nowhere to be found.

THE KNIGHT BEAT

The Knight Beat was right on the floor, not a high stage. Just about a step up, like a sidewalk, maybe a little higher. It was circular and you had people standing all around and in back of wherever you were. After the show you could have chicken or fish or drinks and when the show started you had the entertainers getting dinner right next to you. You know I saw Dinah Washington there. I saw Little Richard. I saw Willie John, Lloyd Price. Everybody. Man. Could you imagine? It was an honor when Sam and Dave got to be a name that we were booked at the Knight Beat. You could hit me in the butt with a shotgun, oh my gawd, to be playing the Knight Beat and the Harlem Square. I was standing on the stage where all the big time entertainers played on. Got my hair processed and all. Seen Sammy Davis Jr, Nat King Cole, Roy Hamilton. Dave and I both wanted to do the best job we could. We were never satisfied just doing what we were supposed to do. We had to do that and more. We wanted to please the audience. That was the main thing, and to please each other. That's what it was all about with us. Ray Charles, and Sam Cooke, and anybody that was ever big time, I saw right there in Overtown. Nappy Brown, "Night Time Is The Right Time," Ruth Brown. I was in amongst all of that. And there are theater signs and photos of a lot of it. There are photos of all the singers and performers that opened for Sam and Dave. I had forgotten about all that until I went down to Miami to do a show for this club and be interviewed for a documentary and they had all these pictures and I stood there and looked at the wall and I was just amazed. From Aretha Franklin to, everybody, they all opened for us when they came to our town. Chuck Jackson opened for Sam And Dave, Otis Redding opened for us at the Miami Stadium. The Staples Singers.... That's why I never understand why they don't invite Sam and Dave to the BET Awards. It hurt, man, but I always feel like I'm giving my best. Promoters are always like can we just use the name Sam and Dave on the marquee? But it's me, Sam Moore, and I've never got the respect that I so dearly believe I deserve. I stopped doing interviews because people just want to know who I slept with, or if I could get Bruce Springsteen for them. And I'm just so tired of that. It's been about 70 years now and Sam and Dave were one of the first groups, duos, that ever made it out of Miami. And it's been 70 years of this stuff. And when thcy say Sam Moore, they call me when they want someone to look good in the audience, or to come to fight night for the Champ. We have been through the walls to get recognized and get the respect to have our labor recognized. And when Jerry Wexler from Atlantic Records took my project and shelved it after Sam and Dave split up in 1969, after King Curtis got murdered, after Brad Shapiro cut a couple sides for it, after Aretha Franklin did her only session playing for anybody else, they robbed me of my solo career. Jerry Wexler robbed me right in 1971 when everybody was leaving their groups. Smoky was leaving the Miracles, Diana Ross left the Supremes, Lionel Richie left the Commodores. My album was brilliant, but Jerry Wexler put it in the vault and forced me back with Dave and that's what took me and sent me over the edge and almost destroyed me with drugs. It was really tough, but I finally got the rights to it and got the album out in 2002, Sam Moore - Plenty Good Lovin': The Lost Solo Album. Then later, Jerry Wexler broke down sobbing when he realized what he'd done to fuck me over. Miami made me. And I left, but you know what? I'm gonna come back and give it the respect and love that the city always had for me.

MUHAMMAD ALI STORY

Champ was down in Miami, and Jackie Wilson, Sam Cooke, Malcolm X, Billy Eckstine, and myself were on 9th street at Nat's Barbershop in Overtown. They all knew me and we were all joking and laughing and then the Champ came in. Cassius Clay. He had just won the Olympics in Rome. It was 1960. I didn't like him at all. He was bragging about he was gonna be this and do that. He was a tall good lookin fella and I just could not stand his ass. He was on and on about "My name is Cassius Clay," and he was punching at the wall and Jackie Wilson was kissing his ass. And then Jackie said, "This is Sam from Sam and Dave," and the Champ said, "Well what song do they have?" and Jackie said, "Well, nothing." And everybody laughed and he was fast as lightning throwing those punches at the wall talking about, "I'm gonna knock out Sonny Liston." And I was just getting mad looking at him and he said,

"Well, what's your problem?" I said, "I don't like you." And everybody in the barbershop know I got a mouth on me, and they say, "Sam, Sam, Sam, calm down, man." I told Clay, "You gonna get your punk ass whooped." He said, "You wanna come to the fight?" And meanwhile Joe Louis was down at the restaurant on the corner having lunch. I said, "Yeah, I wanna go to thc fight. Liston gonna knock your dick out your pants." So they had some tickets brought over to Nat's and we went to the Continental Club, and later went to the beach to go watch the fight. Everybody was there. Somebody gave me some money to go get some stuff, I missed the opening fights, and I got back and I said, "Clay gon get his ass fucked up." And I set my soda down and put a magazine under my ass and as I was leaning down everybody jumped up to look and I said, "What happened?!?" And they say, "Clay just knocked that man out cold." And everybody started teasing me. And this group of guys could tease you so bad you didn't even want to fight. I had to stay off 9th street for a long time after that. Gotdamn they teased me.

One day I went to go get a hair cut from Nat and when I walked in everybody say, "Hey, come here punk!" I said, "Fuck y'all" And they said, "Nah, fuck you!" And then Sam Cooke and I became friends and we were all together all the time down there. And when the

Muslim thing came in Champ got to be a good friend of mine and he would come to the club and say, "Hey, you owe me a song." I owe him every time, and I pay him every time. And that's how we came to be such good friends to this day.

Joyce Moore

Sam Moore's Wife, July 2015

Even though the Champ has some really good days, and some really bad days, when he sees Sam, he still gets a twinkle in his eye. And up until he got sick it was always a comedy show when they were together. When you see the two of them you can just see the love and warmth and friendship that goes back all that time. And Sam will still go up and hug and kiss him on the top of his head and put his arms around his neck and hold him and love on him. It's really something. And the Champ's face lights up with joy.

JOYCE MOORE

Joyce is Sam Moore's wife and manager, and has worked on behalf of artists getting treated right for her entire life.

Interview at Bagel Emporium - 9/30/2023
Questions redacted for narrative flow

"People forget about the hijacking. Flip was on the flight that got hijacked to Cuba. He really was.

He had a sense of timing that was incredible.

I got to see him in different situations and in working with him on the tv show. I wrote a couple jokes, but the first time I ever saw Flip I peed in my pants. I was pregnant. I can tell you when and where.

I was pregnant with my daughter. I was at home with her father, at the time my husband. Flip was on the Johnny Carson show. That was the first time I saw him. 1966. He told the joke about the train conductor and the banana for your monkey. I laughed so hard. When you're pregnant, you pee. The first time I ever met him was at Mr. Kelly's in Chicago. I was the Assistant Maitre D'.

He was headlining. I introduced myself to Flip after rehearsals. I said, "I have a bone to pick with you," he said, "Oh?" y'know and got that look in his eye. I said, "You made me pee my pants."

He said, "What, when??"

I told him the story, and from that moment I was endeared. That endeared me to him. I never laughed so hard…. "And I'll get a banana for your monkey, lady!!" So funny.

His sense of timing was uncanny. And I worked with a lot of comedians. At Mr. Kelly's in Chicago I got to know Alan Sherman, Shelly Berman, Shecky Green, Stu Gilliam, Scoee Mitchell, Flip Wilson, Bill Cosby. Cosby and I were very, very good friends.

My heart breaks for what happened to him. Oh, if you knew all the stories. He got set up by this punk ass District Attorney after everything. He got in a lot of trouble after he got turned out after the sex stuff. They were all doing Quaaludes at the time and stuff. And he got turned out. And that's what started it. That's kinda what happened. He went through a phase where he was absolutely an animal. He was a dog. He was a dawg and just about anything was fair game. And the result unfortunately doesn't justify or make it right, but what the girl and the DA did, at the point in time it happened is when Obama was rising and they had to kill Cosby's message to black youth about the bullshit, about pull your pants up, be proud. Being black doesn't make you a victim.

It was not exactly a conspiracy, but it was deliberate and purposeful. The District Attorney in Philadelphia was a Democrat.

I'm from Chicago but I went to University of Miami and I got to see a comedy sort of band called Doug Clark and The Hot Nuts.

They played all the fraternity parties in 1962, '63, '64, when I was there. They were from the Carolinas, from the beach music scene. They played every frat party up and down the coast. "See the girl all dressed in green. She goes down like a submarine….Hot nut, hot nuts, get em' from the peanut man" and "Let Me Bang Your Box," songs like that.

When Sam (Moore) went solo in 1972, he should have been as big as Marvin Gaye. And Jerry Wexler robbed him because he put his solo album away for thirty years. Jerry Wexler cried about it. Cried and apologized, "What have I done?! Oh no, I'm so sorry…" We have it all on camera.

What Jerry did to Sam, Jerry went to his grave apologizing for. What happened was when Only The Strong came out (2002 soul music documentary), we went to a screening of it at the Hamptons Film Festival. Jerry Wexler was there and when Sam came on screen and started singing "When Something Is Wrong With My Baby," Jerry started bawling. Literally crying like a baby. "Oh my heaven what did I do!? Oy gevalt!" He realized how brilliant Sam was and he put his arms up and was sobbing. He was saying, "Oh what did I do, what did I do to this man?" And I said, "Jerry, Sam's out here in the lobby." He said, "I gotta tell him I'm sorry." Bawling. Blubbering. We go out and Sam is standing there and Wexler runs over to him saying, "Oh, I'm so sorry." Jojo Pennebaker was filming and we have footage of all of this. Jerry was saying, "How, why, I stole from you. I cheated you. I robbed you of your career. Oh, what did I do." Then he and Sam hugged it out. Sam said, "You didn't know. I tried to tell you. You didn't believe me. But you know what, we're ok. Whatever happened, happened. We can't change that."

I wound up speaking at Jerry Wexler's eulogy. I told the whole story there in front of Clive Davis, Ahmet Ertegun, oh yeah, all the boys.

Lenny Bruce? I knew Lenny's mom very well and his daughter. After Lenny died they lived at the Sunset Marquis in LA and she raised Lenny's daughter. So I knew them very well.

I knew all the comedians. Myron Cohen…Mr. Kellys was the premier nightclub in Chicago. There was no Mr. Kelly it was just the name of the place. The owner was George Marienthal. Jews. George and Oscar Marienthal. They opened the Happy Medium, Mr. Kelly's, and the London House, which was the jazz club in Chicago. They owned the three top venues.

Comedy is a problem right now cause you can't be funny. Dave Chappelle and Chris Rock and some of the guys are getting away with it. But it's not like it was, all this stuff with the 'you can't offend.' None of the comedy, the tv, can you imagine *All In The Family* or *Th e Jeffersons* today, there's no fuckin' way.

It's underground.

People are desperate to be entertained and laugh and enjoy, but it's not simple and easy.

That's the thing. There's a void. People think they know and they don't.

I happen to have been there.

Alan Sherman, Shecky Green, Jackie Gayle, Jackie Leonard, Jackie Mason.

Jackie used to call me Little Miss Fuccacio.

All the guys that played. Mort Sahl. I knew all those guys. I knew all of them. That was Chicago.

Miami, it really wasn't segregated. When I went to the University of Miami, we used to go Overtown all the time.

THANKS FOR READING
STAY TUNED FOR MORE

www.ingramcontent.com/pod-product-compliance
Ingram Content Group UK Ltd.
Pitfield, Milton Keynes, MK11 3LW, UK
UKHW042015290726
14061UKWH00001BB/1

9 798218 491512